SOFTWARE ENGINEERING

AUTHOR

Prof. Salman Abdul Moiz

Professor

School of Computer & Information Sciences

University of Hyderabad

REVIEWER

Prof. Rajib Mall

Professor

Department of Computer Science & Engineering

IIT, Kharagpur

KHANNA BOOK PUBLISHING CO. (P) Ltd.

4C/4344, Ansari Road, Darya Ganj, New Delhi, India

All India Council for Technical Education

Nelson Mandela Marg, Vasant Kunj, New Delhi, India

Dear Readers,

To prevent the piracy, this book is secured with HIGH SECURITY HOLOGRAM on the front title cover. In case you don't find the hologram on the front cover title, please write us to at contact@khannabooks.com or whatsapp us at +91-99109 09320 and avail special gift voucher for yourself.

Specimen of Hologram on front Cover title:

Moreover, there is a SPECIAL DISCOUNT COUPON for you with EVERY HOLOGRAM.

How to avail this SPECIAL DISCOUNT:

Step 1: Scratch the hologram

Step 2: Under the scratch area, your "coupon code" is available

Step 3: Logon to www.khannabooks.com

Step 4: Use your "coupon code" in the shopping cart and get your copy at a special discount

Step 5: Enjoy your reading!

ISBN: *978-93-5538-747-9*

Book Code: DIP473EN

Software Engineering

by Prof. Salman Abdul Moiz

First Edition: 2026

Originally Published by:
All India Council for Technical Education, Ministry of Education, GOI

Exclusively Published & Distributed by:
Khanna Book Publishing Co. (P) Ltd.
4C/4344, Ansari Road, Daryaganj,
New Delhi (INDIA)

Visit us at: **www.khannabooks.com**
Write us at: **contact@khannabooks.com**

To view complete list of books, Please scan the QR Code:	KPH

Printed in Bharat.

प्रो. टी. जी. सीताराम
अध्यक्ष
Prof. T. G. Sitharam
Chairman

सत्यमेव जयते

आज़ादी का अमृत महोत्सव

अखिल भारतीय तकनीकी शिक्षा परिषद्
(भारत सरकार का एक सांविधिक निकाय)
(शिक्षा मंत्रालय, भारत सरकार)
नेल्सन मंडेला मार्ग, वसंत कुंज, नई दिल्ली–110070
दूरभाष : 011–26131498
ई–मेल : chairman@aicte-india.org

ALL INDIA COUNCIL FOR TECHNICAL EDUCATION
(A STATUTORY BODY OF THE GOVT. OF INDIA)
(Ministry of Education, Govt. of India)
Nelson Mandela Marg, Vasant Kunj, New Delhi-110070
Phone : 011-26131498
E-mail : chairman@aicte-india.org

FOREWORD

Engineers are the backbone of any modern society. They are the ones responsible for the marvels as well as the improved quality of life across the world. Engineers have driven humanity towards greater heights in a more evolved and unprecedented manner.

The All India Council for Technical Education (AICTE), have spared no efforts towards the strengthening of the technical education in the country. AICTE is always committed towards promoting quality Technical Education to make India a modern developed nation emphasizing on the overall welfare of mankind.

An array of initiatives has been taken by AICTE in last decade which have been accelerated now by the National Education Policy (NEP) 2020. The implementation of NEP under the visionary leadership of Hon'ble Prime Minister of India envisages the provision for education in regional languages to all, thereby ensuring that every graduate becomes competent enough and is in a position to contribute towards the national growth and development through innovation & entrepreneurship.

One of the spheres where AICTE had been relentlessly working since past couple of years is providing high quality original technical contents at Under Graduate & Diploma level prepared and translated by eminent educators in various Indian languages to its aspirants. For students pursuing 2nd year of their Engineering education, AICTE has identified 87 books, which shall be translated into 12 Indian languages - Hindi, Tamil, Gujarati, Odia, Bengali, Kannada, Urdu, Punjabi, Telugu, Marathi, Assamese & Malayalam. In addition to the English medium, books in different Indian Languages are going to support the students to understand the concepts in their respective mother tongue.

On behalf of AICTE, I express sincere gratitude to all distinguished authors, reviewers and translators from the renowned institutions of high repute for their admirable contribution in a record span of time.

AICTE is confident that these outcomes based original contents shall help aspirants to master the subject with comprehension and greater ease.

T.G. Sitharam

(Prof. T. G. Sitharam)

ACKNOWLEDGEMENT

The author is grateful to the authorities of AICTE, particularly Prof. T. G Sitharam, Chairman; Dr. Abhay Jere, Vice-Chairman; Prof. Rajive Kumar, Member-Secretary, and Dr. Ramesh Unnikrishnan, Advisor-II for their support to publish the book on Software Engineering. I would also like to thank Prof. Anil D. Sahasrabudhe, Former Chairman; Prof. M. P. Poonia, Former Vice-Chairman; and Dr. Amit Kumar Srivastava, Former Director of the Faculty Development Cell, for the initial planning of the book.

I sincerely acknowledge the valuable contributions of book reviewer, Prof. Rajib Mall, Professor, Department of Computer Science & Engineering, IIT Kharagpur. His timely suggestions helped make the book students friendly and provide a better shape in an artistic manner.

I want to thank Dean, School of Computer & Information Sciences, University of Hyderabad, and my colleagues for their support from time to time. I thank the Vice Chancellor of University of Hyderabad for allowing me to take up the assignment.

This book is an outcome of various suggestions of AICTE members, experts, and authors who shared their opinion and thought to develop the engineering education in our country further. Acknowledgments are due to the contributors and different workers in this field whose published books, review articles, papers, photographs, footnotes, references, and other valuable information enriched us when writing the book.

Prof. Salman Abdul Moiz

PREFACE

The book "Software Engineering" results from the rich experience teaching basic Software Engineering and allied courses. The initiation of writing this book is to present basic concepts and techniques of software engineering that enable students to get an insight into the subject. The book's contents help students develop a software system by following a systematic approach. The topics recommended by AICTE are included in an organized and orderly manner throughout the book. Efforts have been made to explain the fundamental concepts of the subject in the simplest possible way.

While preparing the manuscript, I have considered the various standard textbooks and the sections like multiple choice questions, short and long questions, etc. While preparing the different sections, emphasis has also been laid on the design and development principles of software systems. The book covers several case studies and metrics that have been presented logically and systematically. This will help students in developing software systems systematically.

Apart from illustrations and examples as required, the book is enriched with numerous solved examples and problems for proper understanding of the related topics. The book consists of five units. The first unit, "Software Development Process," covers the basic concepts of software development and process models. Agile process models, which are required for rapid application development, are presented with a case study. The second unit, "Requirements Engineering," includes the requirements engineering process and the various paradigms of analysis, which is explained through a case study. The Third unit, "Software Design", presents design concepts, software architectures, their applicability, and different software design paradigms with the help of a case study. The unit on "Software Testing" presents concepts, techniques, and approaches to testing a software system. The final unit on "Project Management" describes the tools and techniques for effective software planning and project management. It is essential to note in every chapter, relevant practicals are included. In addition, the "Know More" section presents some additional information on the given topic.

I sincerely hope that the book will inspire the students to learn and discuss the ideas behind basic software engineering principles and will indeed contribute to developing a solid foundation for the subject. I am thankful for all the beneficial comments and suggestions that will contribute to the improvement of the future editions of the book. It gives me immense pleasure to place this book in the hands of the teachers and students. Working on different aspects covered in the book was a great pleasure.

Prof. Salman Abdul Moiz

OUTCOME BASED EDUCATION

For the implementation of an outcome based education the first requirement is to develop an outcome based curriculum and incorporate an outcome based assessment in the education system. By going through outcome based assessments, evaluators will be able to evaluate whether the students have achieved the outlined standard, specific and measurable outcomes. With the proper incorporation of outcome based education there will be a definite commitment to achieve a minimum standard for all learners without giving up at any level. At the end of the programme running with the aid of outcome based education, a student will be able to arrive at the following outcomes:

Programme Outcomes (POs) are statements that describe what students are expected to know and be able to do upon graduating from the program. These relate to the skills, knowledge, analytical ability attitude and behaviour that students acquire through the program. The POs essentially indicate what the students can do from subject-wise knowledge acquired by them during the program. As such, POs define the professional profile of an engineering diploma graduate.

National Board of Accreditation (NBA) has defined the following seven POs for an Engineering diploma graduate:

PO1. Basic and Discipline specific knowledge: Apply knowledge of basic mathematics, science and engineering fundamentals and engineering specialization to solve the engineering problems.

PO2. Problem analysis: Identify and analyses well-defined engineering problems using codified standard methods.

PO3. Design/ development of solutions: Design solutions for well-defined technical problems and assist with the design of systems components or processes to meet specified needs.

PO4. Engineering Tools, Experimentation and Testing: Apply modern engineering tools and appropriate technique to conduct standard tests and measurements.

PO5. Engineering practices for society, sustainability and environment: Apply appropriate technology in context of society, sustainability, environment and ethical practices.

PO6. Project Management: Use engineering management principles individually, as a team member or a leader to manage projects and effectively communicate about well-defined engineering activities.

PO7. Life-long learning: Ability to analyse individual needs and engage in updating in the context of technological changes.

COURSE OUTCOMES

By the end of the course the students are expected to learn:

CO-1: Study software engineering preliminaries and software development process models

CO-2: Apply requirements engineering to software systems

CO-3: Describe software architectures and styles

CO-4: Describe UI design and effective coding techniques

CO-5: Study testing techniques and project management concepts.

Mapping of Course Outcomes with Programme Outcomes to be done according to the matrix given below:

Course Outcomes	Expected Mapping with Programme Outcomes (1- Weak Correlation; 2- Medium correlation; 3- Strong Correlation)						
	PO-1	PO-2	PO-3	PO-4	PO-5	PO-6	PO-7
CO-1	3	2	1	1	3	1	3
CO-2	3	3	3	1	2	2	2
CO-3	3	2	3	2	3	2	3
CO-4	3	3	2	3	1	2	3
CO-5	3	2	2	2	3	3	3

GUIDELINES FOR TEACHERS

To implement Outcome Based Education (OBE) knowledge level and skill set of the students should be enhanced. Teachers should take a major responsibility for the proper implementation of OBE. Some of the responsibilities (not limited to) for the teachers in OBE system may be as follows:

- Within reasonable constraint, they should manoeuvre time to the best advantage of all students.
- They should assess the students only upon certain defined criterion without considering any other potential ineligibility to discriminate them.
- They should try to grow the learning abilities of the students to a certain level before they leave the institute.
- They should try to ensure that all the students are equipped with the quality knowledge as well as competence after they finish their education.
- They should always encourage the students to develop their ultimate performance capabilities.
- They should facilitate and encourage group work and team work to consolidate newer approach.
- They should follow Blooms taxonomy in every part of the assessment.

Bloom's Taxonomy

Level	Teacher should Check	Student should be able to	Possible Mode of Assessment
Create	Students ability to create	Design or Create	Mini project
Evaluate	Students ability to justify	Argue or Defend	Assignment
Analyse	Students ability to distinguish	Differentiate or Distinguish	Project/Lab Methodology
Apply	Students ability to use information	Operate or Demonstrate	Technical Presentation/ Demonstration
Understand	Students ability to explain the ideas	Explain or Classify	Presentation/Seminar
Remember	Students ability to recall (or remember)	Define or Recall	Quiz

GUIDELINES FOR STUDENTS

Students should take equal responsibility for implementing the OBE. Some of the responsibilities (not limited to) for the students in OBE system are as follows:

- Students should be well aware of each UO before the start of a unit in each and every course.
- Students should be well aware of each CO before the start of the course.
- Students should be well aware of each PO before the start of the programme.
- Students should think critically and reasonably with proper reflection and action.
- Learning of the students should be connected and integrated with practical and real life consequences.
- Students should be well aware of their competency at every level of OBE.

ABBREVIATIONS

General Terms			
Abbreviations	**Full form**	**Abbreviations**	**Full form**
SE	Software Engineering	COTS	Commercially Off The Shelf System
IEEE	Institute of Electrical & Electronics Engineers	CBSD	Component Based Software Development
UML	Unified Modelling Language	SRS	Software Requirements Specification
OOAD	Object Oriented Analysis & Design	SSAD	Structured System Analysis & Design
CRC	Class Responsibility Collaboration	CLI	Command Line Interface
UI	User Interface	GUI	Graphical User Interface
MVC	Model View Controller	HTTP	Hyper Text Transfer Protocol
OOA	Object Oriented Analysis	OOD	Object Oriented Design
DFD	Data Flow Diagram	SDD	Software Design Document
TFD	Test First Development	CFG	Control Flow Graph
QA	Quality Assurance	QC	Quality Control
SQA	Software Quality Assurance	SPM	Software Project Management
PMI	Project Management Institute	SCM	Software Configuration Management
LOC	Lines of Code	FP	Function Point
DSI	Delivered Source Code Instructions	KLOC	Kilo Lines of Code
KDSI	Kilo Delivered Source Code Instructions	SLOC	Source Lines of Code
UFP	Unadjusted Function Point	TCF	Technical Complexity Factor
EI	External Inputs	EO	External Outputs

General Terms			
Abbreviations	**Full form**	**Abbreviations**	**Full form**
I	Inquiries	IF	Internal Files
EF	External Files	CAF	Complexity Adjustment Factor
PM	Person-Months	COCOMO	Constrictive Cost Model
WBS	Work Breakdown Structure	MT	Minimum Time
EST	Earliest Start Time	EFT	Earliest Finish Time
LFT	Latest Finish Time	ST	Slack Time
LST	Latest Start Time	ACT	Annual Change Traffic
SCM	*Software Configuration* Management	SCI	Software Configuration Item
CCA	Change Control Authority	ECO	Engineering Change Order
XP	Extreme Programming	MR	Modification Request

LIST OF FIGURES

Unit 1 Software Development Life Cycle

Unit 2 Requirements Engineering

Unit 4 Testing

CONTENTS

Unit 4: Software Testing 106-137

1 Software Development Process

UNIT SPECIFICS

In this unit, we have discussed the following aspects:

- *Fundamentals of software engineering;*
- *Challenges in software development;*
- *Software development activities;*
- *Generic software development process models;*
- *Iterative software development process models;*
- *Agile process model;*

The practical applications of the topics are discussed for generating further curiosity and creativity as well as improving problem solving capacity.

Besides giving multiple choice questions as well as questions of short and long answer types marked in two categories following lower and higher order of Bloom's taxonomy, assignments, a list of references and suggested readings are given in the unit so that one can go through them for practice. It is important to note that for getting more information on various topics of interest some QR codes have been provided in different sections which can be scanned for relevant supportive knowledge.

After the related practical, based on the content, there is a "Know More" section. This section has been carefully designed so that the supplementary information provided in this part becomes beneficial for the users of the book. This section mainly highlights the initial activity, examples of some interesting facts, analogy, history of the development of the subject focusing the salient observations and finding, timelines starting from the development of the concerned topics up to the recent time, applications of the subject matter for our day-to-day real life or/and industrial applications on variety of aspects, case study related to environmental, sustainability, social and ethical issues whichever applicable, and finally inquisitiveness and curiosity topics of the unit.

RATIONALE

The initial era of Computers in the mid- 1960s was essentially known as the programming era because computer coding was reaping significant benefits at that time. Computations were done faster with the help of programming languages like Fortran etc. With the increase in computing power, the demands of the industry also increased. Thereby the complexity of the program increased further. It was challenging to manage the complexity of systems.

In 1963, the time-sharing systems came into existence [McCarthy]. Unlike batch processing systems, these systems provided greater interactivity. The transition from batch processing to time-sharing systems increased the complexity of the programs. The systems at that time were typically prone to two major issues. First, the product delivery was delayed, and the cost increased. Second, there were operational issues in dealing with this transition. Major organizations were affected by this transition and were either closed or on the verge of a major collapse.

In 1968, NATO sponsored a conference in which the issues faced by the organizations were openly discussed for the first time. The terms "Software Engineering" and "Software Crisis" were coined during the conference. It was resolved that the current software development practices are inadequate, and new methodologies and mechanisms have to be adopted for the development of a software.

In the last 5 to 6 decades, there have been several changes in technological aspects which also changes methods, processes, and techniques for developing software systems. To benchmark these processes several standards and assessment methods were developed over a period which requires continuous changes. Hence the technological transitions have to be guided by proper processes, methods, assessment strategies and standards which form the building blocks of Software Engineering.

In this unit, students get a primary idea about the basic concepts of software engineering. It initially presents the technical jargon used in software development. The next part of this unit deals with understanding the software process and various software development activities.
The Generic, Iterative and Agile software development models are explained. The advantages and disadvantages of these models are highlighted. This unit also presents the applicability of these process models to various domains.

PRE-REQUISITES

Computer Programming (Diploma Semester-III)

Scripting Languages (Diploma Semester-III)

UNIT OUTCOMES

List of outcomes of this unit is as follows:

U1-O1: Describe the basic concepts of software development,

U1-O2: Describe the challenges in software development

U1-O3: Describe Generic and Iterative software development models

U1-O4: Assess suitability of software development models for various applications

Unit-1 Outcomes	EXPECTED MAPPING WITH COURSE OUTCOMES (1- Weak Correlation; 2- Medium correlation; 3- Strong Correlation)				
	CO-1	**CO-2**	**CO-3**	**CO-4**	**CO-5**
U1-O1	3	1	1	-	3
U1-O2	3	2	2	1	2
U1-O3	3	2	2	2	2
U1-O4	3	3	3	2	2

1.1 SOFTWARE ENGINEERING PRELIMINARIES

1.1.1 Software

Software is a system asset that coordinates to realize a task or a goal. The system assets include programs, documentation and mechanisms needed to operate the software system. A holistic view of a software is given in Fig 1.1. The software consists of a set of programs. It also contains a set of documents. These documents are primarily for users and developers of the system. A set of rules to install and use the software are specified in the operational guidelines.

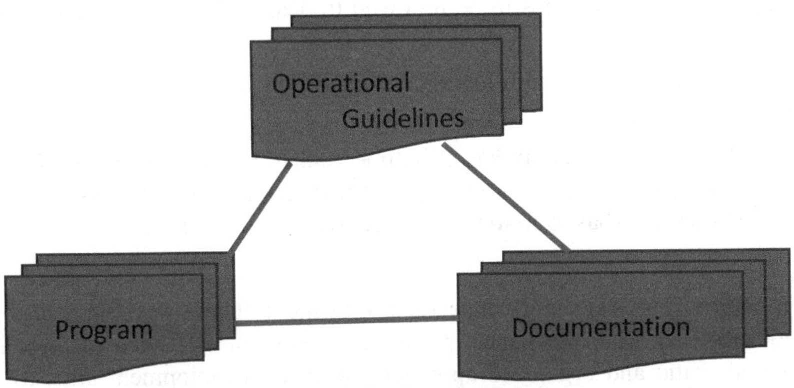

Fig. 1.1: A Holistic view of a Software

The programs include source code and object code. Program typically consists of instructions to execute a particular task. For the successful development of a program, it has to go through various steps, and each step has to be properly documented. This documentation will be needed to understand the program better and make necessary changes when desired.

A particular set of guidelines has to be adopted to make the software operational. This is provided in the form of manuals. Generally, there are two types of manuals, viz. - Developer and user manual. A Developer manual helps programmers and developers understand the systems design and implementation. This manual will help the developers maintain the system in the future. The user manual specifies the steps to use the system.

In summary, the software alone will not help the users. In addition, we need procedures to operate and a mechanism to assist end users in using the software effectively. For example, if one has to install BOSS (Bharat Operating System Solutions), one must know the steps to install and operate it. In addition, we need documentation to use the open-source operating system.

1.1.2 Software Engineering

The term software engineering came into existence to deal with the software crisis. In 1968 it was felt that Software development is an engineering discipline where each step in software development should be realized by following well-defined principles and practices.

As per IEEE, "*Software Engineering is a systematic approach for development, operation, maintenance and retirement of a software*".

The above definition includes four dimensions:

Development: This process starts with identifying the problem to be solved, understanding, designing, implementing, and testing. These activities are expected to follow well-defined principles.

Operation: The developed software system has to follow certain rules for its installation and use. It also includes the mechanisms to be followed to deal with reliability and other aspects of the system.

Maintenance: The systems modifications must follow a change request process so that the existing functionalities are not affected.

Retirement: Each real-time entity has a lifetime, and so is for the software. Once an application becomes obsolete, it is time to stop using it, but there should be access to historical data. The application closure also has to follow a specific, well-defined process.

Software engineering is not only concerned with the software development, but also includes other activities such as maintenance, project management etc. Each of these activities has to follow a systematic and organized approach. Software development aims to produce quality software within time and given budget. This goal can be achieved by following scientific and proven methods.

1.1.3 Systems Engineering

Systems engineering gives a holistic view of product development. Software alone is insufficient for the realization of goals. Software drives hardware. When the programs are developed and executed, they have to be deployed on a particular machine or device. Process engineering is an engineering discipline used to design, implement and control systems engineering activities. These activities will enable the developers to produce high-quality software.

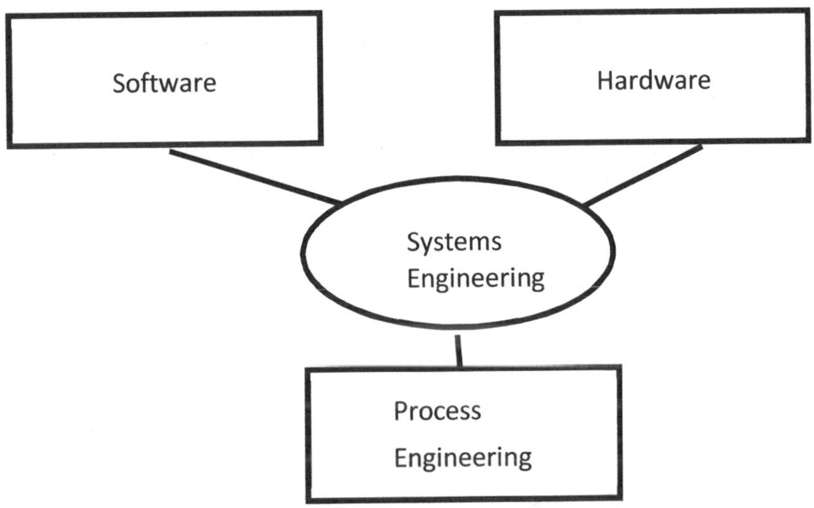

Fig. 1.2: Systems Engineering

Systems engineering includes set of programs written, executed and deployed on a hardware device. This includes computer chip design, spacecraft design etc.

Computer sciences is a branch of study that deals with theory and fundamentals. Software engineering deals with mechanisms for developing and delivering useful software products.
As per the traditional practices, software engineering has to be supported by the concept of computer science, but due to various factors faced by industry and customer demands, this is not the reality. Software engineering sometimes may have to adopt ad-hoc approaches for developing software.

1.1.4 4P's of Software Development

Traditionally there are 4P's used in software development domain. They are

- Process
- People
- Project
- Product

A *Process* refers to a sequence of activities producing an outcome. Software process refers to activities that interact to produce a software product.
Each activity in a process takes certain inputs and produces an outcome. These outcomes are often referred to as *artifacts*. Each process or activity has to satisfy specific criteria before the process or activity starts. This activity is known as Pre-condition. Each activity has to satisfy its *pre-condition* for its execution to produce an artifact. In the software process, each of these outcomes may be documentation, source code, test result, etc.

For example, each university or institution possesses an admission process. The admission process consists of a particular sequence of activities. Though the admission process differs from one institution to another, it usually starts with a student applying for a specific course until they get a course allotment or get rejected. Each of these activities has to satisfy a pre-condition to realize the same. To apply to a particular course, a student has to either pass the qualifying exam or might have appeared for the qualifying exam. This acts as a pre-condition.

After applying for a particular course, the student receives an acknowledgment in the form of a registration number or a receipt. This is the artifact for the first activity. Similarly, all activities produce different artifacts.

Any development or production activity needs *People*. They are required at all levels, from a manager to a helper. A specific set of people must carry out each activity in the software development process. People are identified by their roles. Figure 1.3 specifies the relationship between people (Specified by role), activity, artifact, and process. Programmers and Testers (People) are responsible for Implementation and Testing (Activities) to produce Source code and Test reports (Artifacts)

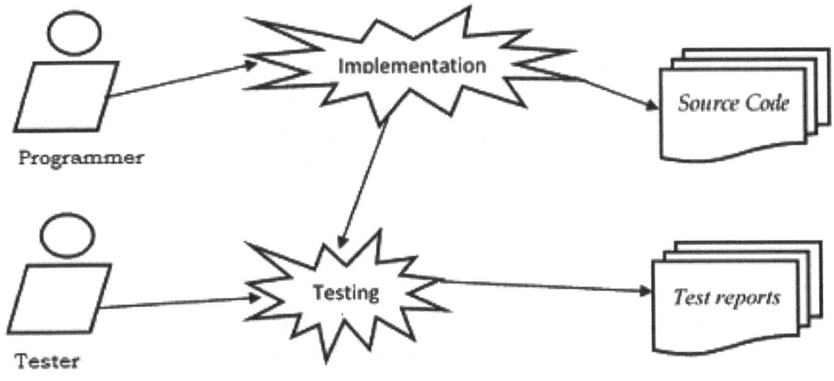

Fig. 1.3: Role, activity and artifacts

It is evident from fig 1.3 that first implementation activity is realized, then the testing activity. This sequence of activities forms a process.

The *Product* is the final outcome of the process. The artifacts or deliverables produced by each activity together constitute a product. In software development process, documentation, source code, object code, and test reports are the final artifacts needed. They are subsets of the final product.

Project covers planning and project management activity which is most important to monitor the products development progress. This includes planning, staffing, managing, and directing activities toward the project's development. It is a critical activity as software development is a time-bound activity. This also includes the estimation of cost and time for each of the activities of the product under development.

1.2 CHALLENGES IN SOFTWARE DEVELOPMENT

In the mid-1960s, there were several issues faced by organizations during the development of software. These software crises were discussed at the NATO conference leading to an engineering branch in software development called software engineering. However, new challenges emerge due to the changing nature of software from time to time. A few of the challenges faced by software developers during the last six decades are discussed below:

- *Time and cost overrun:* As software development is time bound, any delay in delivering the software on time also affects its cost. The delay might have resulted because of improper understanding of the requirements, unskilled workforce, lack of adequately defined processes, organizational issues, etc.

- *Communication issues:* These issues are generally observed between the customer, developer, or development team members. The developer's improper understanding of the customer's requirements may lead to erroneous product development. Similarly, there could be coordination problems among members of development teams. This usually happens when the development teams are distributed geographically.

- *Lack of quality products*: Ensuring the quality of the developed product is the goal of software engineering. However, product doesn't conform to users requirements due to improper testing. Some software products take an enormous time to ensure software quality, which is not acceptable to the customers.

- *Lack of clarity by customers:* In some scenarios, the customer is not clear about their requirements. In such cases, the end product doesn't meet the customer's expectation.

- *Heterogeneity*: This is one of the critical challenges of software engineering. The current systems are required to operate in a distributed way across networks on different types of machines and devices. There is also a need to integrate the new systems with the legacy systems using different programming languages to work efficiently.

- *Trust*: Trust is an important issue faced by all stakeholders. The system available at the remote station must be trusted by users to access it from any place and from any device.

To address these challenges, new techniques and methods are needed from time to time.

1.3 SOFTWARE QUALITY ATTRIBUTES

Software engineering aims to produce quality product within time and budget. Oxford dictionary defines quality as a "Degree of excellence". According to Edward Deming, quality is defined as "Fitness for the purpose". Generally, a product that is user-friendly and meets the customers' requirements and desired performance requirements is a quality product. Each software product has several associated attributes that define its quality.

- Maintainability: Each software system is prone to changes. Hence software must be built to cope with all future changes. This includes correcting the defects that occurred, modifying the existing elements of the system, and adding new functionalities to the current system.

- Reliability: A system is reliable if it does not produce costly failures. The ability of the product to sustain in the presence of disasters is the reliability of the system. It is the probability that the system will work as expected for a specified time interval.
- Usability: The ability to develop software that is easy to use is the usability of a software. This is possible by providing proper user interfaces. The user interfaces may be designed based on the maturity of target users of the system.
- Efficiency: The ability of software to use optimal resources is its efficiency. It includes memory utilization, processing time, etc.
- Interoperability: The ability of a system or a module to exchange data or services with other module is referred to as interoperability. These modules may work on different operating systems, programming languages, and environments.
- Security: Security ensures that the system or modules are prevented from unauthorized access. It also includes avoiding information loss, protecting the privacy of data and ensuring that the system is virus free.
- Portability: The ability of the systems to work on other platforms or environments.
- Reusability: Reuse helps in producing quality software that is cost-effective and time efficient. The system has to be divided into modules so that these modules are reusable across the applications.

These quality characteristics varies from one system to another. The desired quality attributes have to be identified before developing the system.

1.4 SOFTWARE DEVELOPMENT

Software development includes sequence of activities required to build a software product. This includes designing, developing, testing, and managing a software.

1.4.1 Software Process

Software process refers to the activities used to develop a software system. One may either develop the system from scratch or may request modifications to the existing system.

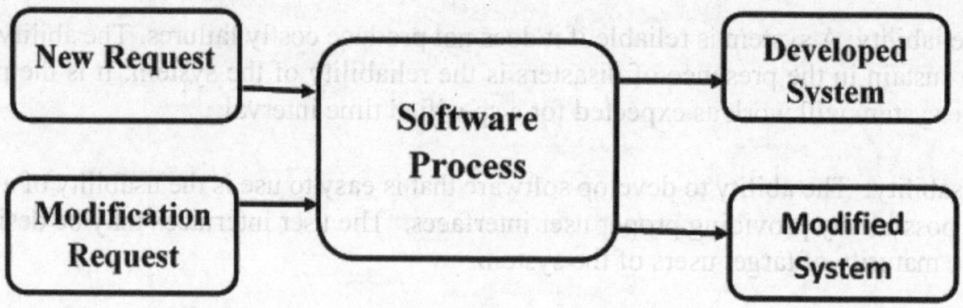

Fig. 1.4: Software Process

An organization may use many processes which are either executed serially or simultaneously. Few of these processes are not concerned with software engineering, but they may impact software development. The software process is the mechanism that deals with technical and managerial issues of software development.

An educational institution may implement several processes. This may include Admission, Teaching-Learning, Examination and Evaluation, Placement etc. The automation of each of these processes has to follow certain software development activities.

There are several generic processes available. However, organizations tend to follow processes suitable to their needs. Irrespective of the software process used, fundamental activities are common across all the processes. The basic software development activities are:

- Requirements Analysis and Specification
- Design and Implementation
- Testing
- Evolution and decommissioning

1.4.2 Requirements Analysis and Specification

The goal of this activity is to collect the requirements from the customer, understand the requirements without any ambiguity and identify the systems constraints that are needed for the operation and deployment of the system. This is an initial and vital phase of development. Any gap in understanding the requirements may affect all the subsequent phases, resulting in a product not satisfying the customer.

There are two levels of requirements. Customers or stakeholders need high-level requirements, whereas developers require detailed system specifications.

Requirements engineering is the process of eliciting requirements, analyzing, specifying, documenting, and validating the same. The requirements engineering process is specified in figure 1.5. The requirements engineering process starts with assessing the project's feasibility, and goes through four phases. The artifacts produced by the requirements engineering process includes Feasibility report and requirements specification document.

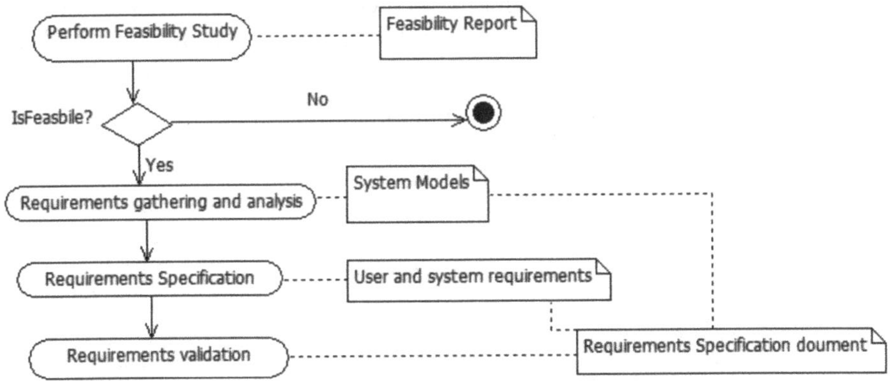

Fig. 1.5: Requirements Engineering Process

In the first phase, a feasibility study is performed, which decides whether to proceed with a detailed requirements analysis. Three types of feasibility is assessed: Technical, Economical, and Operational Feasibility. Technical feasibility ensures whether the required infrastructure (software, hardware) and human resources to develop the system is available or can be hired. Economic feasibility deals with ensuring that the proposed system is cost-effective i.e., it assesses whether the system can be built with the available budget of the organization. Operational feasibility ensures that the system, when developed, will be easy to use by the customers and that the stakeholders will accept the created or modified system. Based on the outcome of the feasibility report, the actual requirements engineering process begins. It is to be noted that the feasibility study phase should be quick and cheap. The artifact of the feasibility study is the feasibility report.

The second phase is the requirements elicitation process, where the requirements are collected from the potential users. The requirements can be collected through Interviews, Questionnaires, reviewing records, and observations. A high-level prototype is developed to understand the system better. To better understand the customer's requirements, models are developed. The artifact of this phase is the System models for the needs collected.

The third phase is the requirement specification. In this phase, the requirements gathered in the analysis phase are translated into a document that signifies a set of requirements. There are two views of the requirements. The first one is the user requirements which are documented for the system's end users. System requirements specify details of the functionality of the system.

The fourth stage is of requirements validation. In this phase, it is checked whether the requirements documented are complete, correct, and unambiguous. If there is any discrepancy, the requirements have to be modified.

1.4.3 Design and Implementation

The design aims to realize the solution for the problem specified by the requirements specification document. This is the first step to realizing solution to the problem domain identified during requirements specification process.

The process of design of a system is depicted in figure 1.6

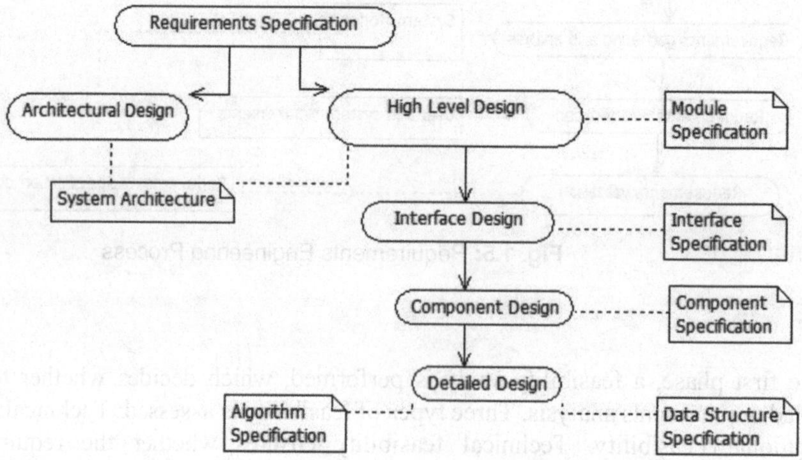

Fig. 1.6: A generic Design Process

In the Architectural design phase, the software system's structure is decided based on the requirements specified. The artifact produced is the architecture of the system. The architecture specifies the structure of the system. The high-level design phase identifies the modules or sub-systems. The specification of each of these modules forms the artifact of this phase. An equivalent interface design is needed for each system and sub-systems identified in the previous phase. These interfaces realize a service of the module or sub-modules. The component design aims at developing sub-systems so that they can be effectively reused across applications. To access these components, we need proper interfaces.

The data structures and algorithms needed to provide the required services are designed in the detailed design phase. The artifacts of the design phase include architecture description, module specification, interface specification, component specification, data structure, and algorithm specification.

The design model varies from one type of paradigm to another. It may adopt structured methods, object-oriented methods, or the agile approach.

Implementation aims to transform the design to source code and test the individual modules or units. Many of the coding decisions depend on the target programming language used. The program has to satisfy the basic features like readability, simplicity, clarity etc. Once programs are written, one needs to thest them to know the defects present if any. This process is called debugging. The goal of testing is to identify the existence of defects, and debugging is the mechanism to locate the error, repair them and test the program again.

1.4.4 Testing

In order to ensure that the system conforms to the specification, verification and validation (V&V) activities need to be carried out. Small programs may be tested as a single unit. However, a typical software system, is expected to carry out testing at three levels: Unit testing, System testing and Acceptance testing as specified in figure 1.7.

In unit testing, individual modules or components are tested independently. These entities could be functions or methods.

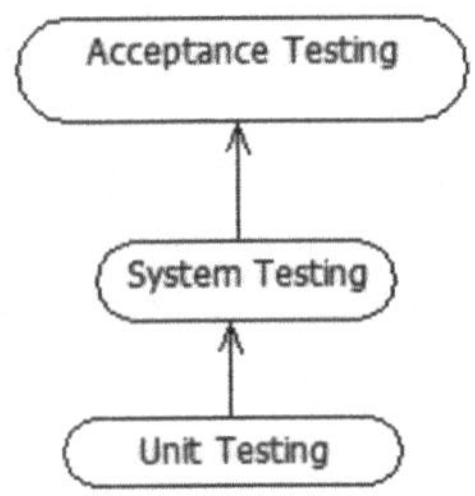

Fig. 1.7: Levels of Testing

In System testing, the individual units are integrated to make up a system and are tested to locate errors if any. Further the system's compliance with that of functional and non-functional requirements is also verified.

In Acceptance testing, the system is tested with real data supplied by the customers or users. During this testing, the user can verify whether the system meets their expectations. Acceptance testing is sometimes called alpha testing.

The test cases for each level of testing can be derived and based on the outcome of testing, test reports are generated.

1.4.5 Evolution and decommissioning

Change is inevitable in most of an organization's technical and mangerial processes. However, there is a need to manage the change requests. Software maintenance or evolution involves the software engineering activities that need to be carried out after the delivery of the software product to the customer. There are three types of maintenance

- Corrective: In this type of maintenance, the system is modified to remove bugs.
- Adaptive: In this type of maintenance, the system has to work on new platforms and environments.
- Perfective: In this type of maintenance, changes may be made to the existing functionalities of the system, or new functionalities may be added.

Change management process is represented in Figure 1.8

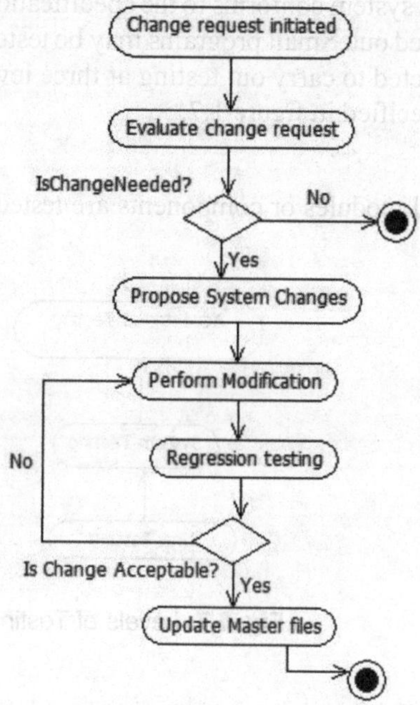

Fig. 1.8: Change Management Process

The change request is evaluated whenever the modification request is initiated to check its need. If the change is not relevant or not immediately desired, then the change request is closed. Otherwise, the expected changes are proposed, and modification is done to the system. Once the changes are realized, regression testing is done to check for any side effects to the system due to modification. Once the regression testing is successful, it is checked whether the changes made to the system are acceptable. If changes are acceptable, the master files are updated, and the process stops.

When the software life cycle completes i.e whenever software becomes obsolete, there is a need to have a proper closure process. The existing software assets have to follow proper discard process. Further, the historical data should be made available for the future systems.

1.4.6 Software Development Process

The objective of software engineering is to deliver the system or product as per the customers' expectations. In addition, the product developed is expected to be of quality which is to be completed within specified time and available budget. This is possible only when a proper, well-defined and appropriate process is realized.

The Software development process is an abstract representation of a software process. The Software Life Cycle refers to the period from its inception till its retirement. In the software development process, the emphasis is on activities related to software production including analysis, design, coding and testing. The importance of such a development process leads to various models being proposed from time to time. The generic activities of process models are discussed in previous section. Software Process models are generally classified into two categories: Generic development process and Iterative development process.

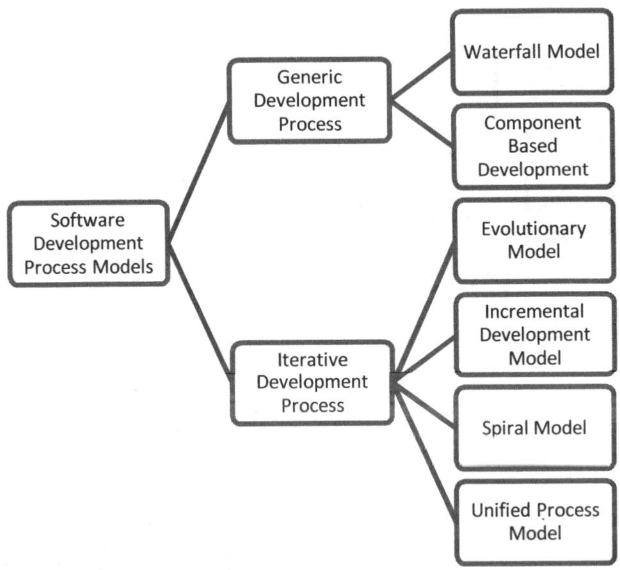

Fig. 1.9: Taxononomy of Software Development Process

The generic software development process model specifies the primary steps to developing the software from scratch or using the already existing systems. In order to address some of the problems of the generic development process, the Iterative development process has evolved. Fig. 1.9 specifies the taxonomy of the software development process models.

1.5 GENERIC DEVELOPMENT PROCESS

Generic development models are widely used in software development. In this section, two generic process models are discussed.

- Waterfall model
- Component based software development

1.5.1 Waterfall Model

The first generic model of software development is the waterfall model. It was first proposed by Royce (1970) in which the phases are organized in a linear order. The variations of this model evolved over a period of time to fit into the defined processes of an organization. The waterfall model is a plan-driven model where each activity is clearly defined and documented. The model is shown in fig. 1.10

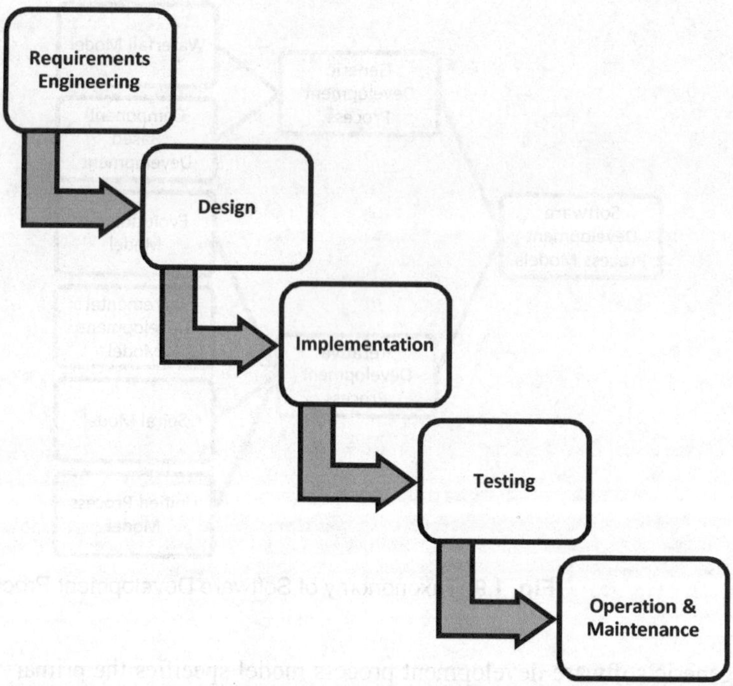

Fig. 1.10: Waterfall Model

In the requirements engineering phase, a feasibility study is carried out. If the project is feasible, then the requirements are gathered. The systems functionality, constraints and goals are identified which are further elaborated to form a requirements specification.

In the design phase, the solution is planned for the problem domain identified during the requirements engineering phase. This includes high-level design and low-level design. The system's architecture is identified, system may be divided into modules, interfaces are defined, algorithms and data structures are defined.

In the implementation, the design is translated into the source code. The programs written depend on the target programming language used. Then the modules of the system are tested to verify whether their functionalities conform to module specifications.

In the testing phase, the individual units of programs are integrated and tested to ensure that the system meets the requirements stated in the beginning. Once beta testing (testing the functionality and other quality requirements like security, reliability etc.), is completed, the system is delivered to the customer.

In the operation and maintenance phase, the system is initially installed and used by the user. During this process, modification requests may be initiated by the system's users. This includes correcting errors, enhancing services, and making changes to the system.

The completion of each phase results in certain artifacts. The waterfall model's next phase doesn't begin until the current phase is freeezed. There is a possibility that during the design, problems with requirements may emerge. Similarly, during coding, design issues may be found etc. Under such a scenario, the waterfall model can't be a simple linear model because the development may not proceed further, and it may be iterated to resolve the issues at one phase or the other.

The advantages of the waterfall model are as follows:

- It is a simple model where the task of building software is divided into well-defined phases, and each phase deals with a specified activity.
- Each phase results in a definite artifact that fits into other engineering processes. For example, the artifact produced from requirements engineering activity includes a feasibility report, requirements specification, and project planning document. The artifacts produced from design activity includes Software design document. The artifact of the Implementation phase includes programs. The artifacts of the testing phase are test plans and test reports. Finally the manuals are prepared for the installation and support activities.
- It is easy to manage and control software development using the waterfall model as each phase is clearly defined, and the artifacts or documents produced by each phase is specified.

The disadvantages of the waterfall model are as follows:

- The software is available for use only after the final phase of the model. The user is not aware of how the software works till it is deployed. If the user is not satisfied, the entire process may have to be repeated resulting in cost and time overrun issues.
- Since requirements are frozen before proceeding to the design phase, subsequent changes to the requirements are challenging to manage. Further, the required hardware is selected at the end of the requirements phase. The hardware may become obsolete for larger systems when the final software is ready to deploy.

The waterfall model can be used when the requirements are complete and consistent and are not-likely to change during the development process. Since the waterfall model resembles other engineering models, it is still a widely used model.

1.5.2 Component Based Software Development

Effective reuse of software assets can enhance the productivity of a system. For rapid system development, it is essential to reuse the system or its modules or functions. Since the reused module or function is properly tested, it reduces effort for development and testing. The development team can use software assets if they are aware of design and code of similar systems. In specific scenarios, the module or function to be reused can be modified to fit the requirements of current system.

Component-based software development or reuse-driven development is the process of developing a system that mainly aims to reuse the existing software assets.

The reuse-oriented software development is expected to maintain a database of reusable software assets or components. This is often referred to as component repository. Such components which are commercially packaged for specific functionality and are available for the industry needs are referred to as commercial off-the-shelf systems (COTS). The component-based software development process is represented in fig 1.11

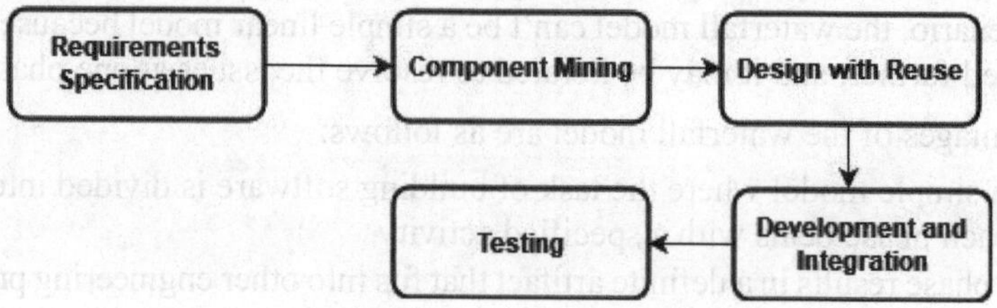

Fig. 1.11: Component Based Development Process

In the first phase requirements, analysis and specification is done to generate requirements specification document. *Given the requirements, a look-up is performed in the component mining* phase to search for a component that satisfies the given specification. The component can be a source code, architecture, design or documentation. There may be a component in the repository which can be used as it is, or its partial functionality could be reused, or there may not be any component satisfying the given requirements. Sometimes requirements are modified based on the available components. If the modifications are not possible, the component repository is searched again to find an alternative solution.

In System design with reuse phase, a new framework is designed, or the existing one is reused. Other new components are designed if the reusable components are not available. They are designed in such a way that they may be reused in future requirements requests. In development and integration phase, software assets that cannot be externally procured are developed, and components of COTS system are integrated to produce a system meeting the requirements. In the testing phase, the developed system is tested with that of requirements specification. During this phase, newly developed components or modules are tested thoroughly, and after integrating the same with other available components or COTS, it is again tested for integration testing and system testing.

Component-based software development has the advantage of rapidly developing software, reduceing the cost of development. This also reduces the testing effort. However, sometimes the system developed may not meet the customers' expectations. Further, the new or modified components stored in the component repository are not in the control of the organizations using them.

1.6 ITERATIVE DEVELOPMENT PROCESS

The activities of process development are not always linear. There is a possibility that some of the process activities may be regularly repeated. This may be needed when the requirements are not precise or when there are changes expected to the requirements specification. The evolutionary, Incremental, spiral, and Unified Process involve iteration of a few of their phases.

1.6.1 Evolutionary Model

This model aims to address a few issues of waterfall model. Instead of freezing the requirements, an initial version of the system is developed using the essential requirements available. At this stage, there is a basic understanding of requirements. However, there is a possibility that new requirements may be included or there is a need for changes to the existing requirements specification.

There are two variants of the evolutionary model:

- Exploratory Development: In this model, the objective is to work with the stakeholders, explore the requirements and deliver the system. The development activity begins when the basic functionalities of the system are understood. The system evolves as the customer requests new features.

- Throwaway prototyping: The throwaway prototype development begins when the preliminary requirement specification document is available. At this stage, there is a possibility that the entire requirements may not be known. Even if the customer or stakeholder cannot give the entire requirements, a prototype can be built with the initial requirements. The activities of the prototyping model are represented in fig 1.12.

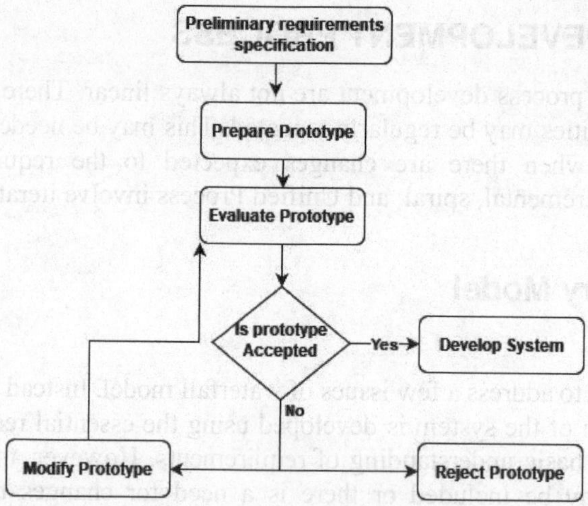

Fig. 1.12: Prototype Model

Once the prototype is developed, it is given to the customer to use and evaluate. The customer may accept the prototype, may request a modification or reject the prototype. The customers continuous feedback helps produce final requirements specification generally known as operational requirements. It may be noted that the prototype is to be developed only for the requirements which are not clear. The requirements which are complete and consistent don't need a prototype. Further minimum documentation is expected in prototyping for rapid development of the software.

The evolutionary model applies to projects where it becomes difficult to determine the requirements and the customer is unclear about the same. The prototype may help in evolving the system over some time.

Generally, there are two problems with evolutionary models. Firstly the evolutionary models may not be suitable for large and complex systems where different teams develop different aspects of the system. It will be challenging to integrate the elements of the system across teams. Secondly, there are issues with managerial aspects. As no definite deliverables are produced, the managers cannot measure the progress of the systems development. It will not be cost-effective to develop documents for system version.

1.6.2 Incremental Development Model

One of the drawbacks of the waterfall model was that by the end of the requirements engineering phase, the requirements are frozen. Whenever a change is requested, it is not possible until the system with current functionality is delivered. These changes can be taken only during maintenance. This increases the cost and time for the development and may produce a software product that may not wholly satisfy customer needs.

The goal of the incremental development model is to manage the requirements changes. It helps the customer to continuously give feedback to the system as it is delivered in parts. An increment is a subset of requirements. In the incremental development process, the requirements are divided into several increments. Each increment is designed, implemented, and tested to produce a build. Each build produces an executable code. This build is now available to the customer to use and give feedback, if any. Other increments are also under development in a pipeline. The subsequent increments are integrated and tested to produce a build that provides a composite functionality of increments. The first increment usually contains the basic functionality to be implemented. The process of incremental development is depicted in figure 1.13.

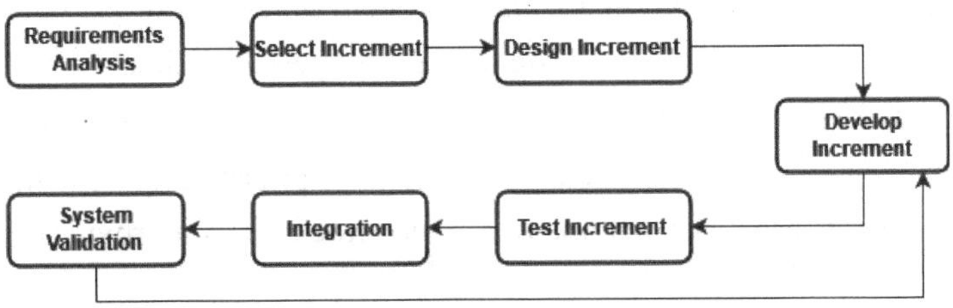

Fig. 1.13: Incremental Development Process

In the first phase, requirements collection and analysis are performed. In the second phase, the basic functionality is selected as an increment from the requirements specification. In the third phase, the increment is designed, and then increment is developed and tested. The tested increment produces a build available for the customer to use and give feedback. In integration phase two builds of increments are integrated and tested. The increments should be planned in such a way that those increments which are not clear or are expected to have several changes are postponed to be taken up later.

The increments are expected to be relatively smaller and has to deliver a functionality. There is a general perception that incremental development process takes more time as each increment has to go through design, development, testing and integration phases. However these increments are realized in a pipeline as depicted in figure 1.14.

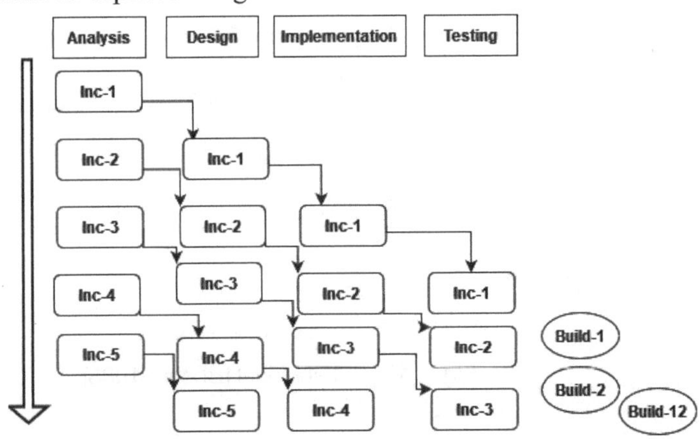

Fig. 1.14: Pipellining mechanism to manage increments

Generally, each activity is carried out by separate teams. For example, analyst, designer, programmer, and tester are usually separate roles. Fig 2.11 shows that at some time during incremental development, entire development team will be executing one task or another. For example, when increment I5 is being analyzed, I4 will be designed, I3 will be under implementation, and I2 in the testing phase. Once an increment is ready, Build1 is available to the customer. Similarly, when Build2 is tested successfully, it is integrated with the previous build, and integration testing is performed.

The advantages of the incremental development model are

- The customer can see part of a working system as few builds are ready.
- Customers can start using the system in a short period of time
- The feedbacks given by the customer may help the later increments.
- Requirements can be prioritized, and the highest priority requirements can be delivered first, and later the subsequent increments are integrated. Thus it provides continuous integration.

1.6.3 Spiral Model

The spiral model combines the good features of the waterfall model and Evolutionary models. It was proposed by Boehm in 1988. In this model, the activities are not organized sequentially. However, they are represented as a spiral, so different alternatives can be planned if needed. The spiral model addresses the risks during software development

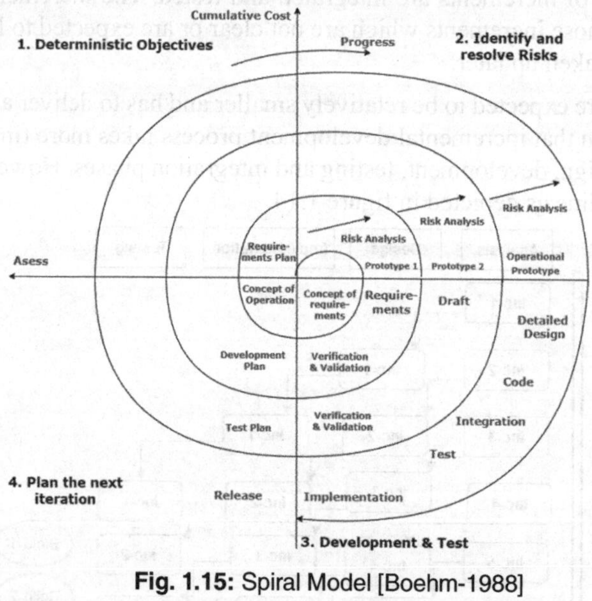

Fig. 1.15: Spiral Model [Boehm-1988]

Spiral model is depicted in figure 1.15 Each cycle in the spiral represents a phase of the software development process. Each cycle begins with the identification of objectives and constraints for each phase. Project risks are identified, and risk aversion strategies are planned. The next step is to perform risk analysis. For each identified risk, necessary steps are to be planned to reduce the risk. For example, if there is a risk that the requirements are unclear, a prototype may be developed.

In the next step, the development model is decided. This depends on the risk evaluation done during the previous step. If there is a risk of integrating the modules, then the waterfall model may be used. If there is a risk involved with a change in requirements, then incremental model may be used etc. In the last step, the project is reviewed and a decision is made to plan the next phase. For example, if the requirements are not validated, the next cycle is planned to improve its prototype.

A risk is the probability that the system results in an organization's potential. The risk may be reduced, but it can't be eliminated. Before a risk actually happens, it's better to know the alternatives to be taken so that they can be realized to reduce the risk. Risk exposure is the measure that can be used to assess the risk in each step.

$$Re = Pr(e) * L$$

Where Re is risk exposure, Pr(e) is the probability of the occurrence of event *e* and *L* is the loss occurred due the risk.

1.6.4 Unified Process Model

The Unified Process model is suitable for modern systems development. It combines the best features of almost all models available in the literature. It brings together advantages of the waterfall model, iterative model, evolutionary model, and incremental model so that the good practices can be adopted. Thus unified process model is sometimes known as a hybrid model. The Unified Process was proposed by Rumbaugh et. Al. (1998-99). The Unified Process supports iterative and incremental development where the development is done in short and fixed intervals called Iterations. Each iteration goes through the primary phases of software development which includes requirements analysis, design, implementation, and testing.

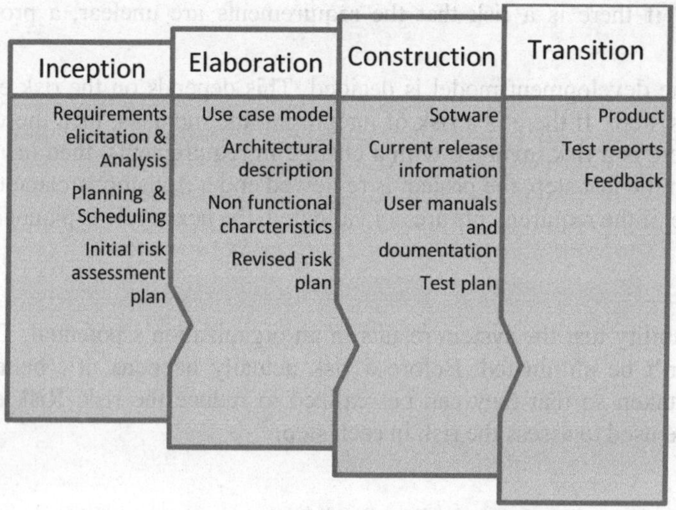

Fig. 1.16: Unified Process

Unified Process has four phases viz Inception, Elaboration, Construction, and Transition, as depicted in the figure 1.16. The goal of the Inception phase is to define the scope of the system. This identifies the entities which are interacting with the system and their responsibilities. In general, the requirements are captured and defined in this phase. The outcome of this phase is to define the objectives of the project clearly.

The goal of the elaboration phase is to understand the problem domain, establish a project plan and define high-level architecture of the system. The milestone of this phase is to produce a lifecycle architecture.

The construction phase deals with design and implementation. The increments can be developed in parallel and integrated. The outcome of this phase is a working software that is ready to be delivered to the customer. The transition phase deals with the operation and deployment of the system in the real-time environment. These four phases constitute the development life cycle.

The Unified Process recommends six best practices referred to as good software engineering practices.

- Develop Iteratively: The increment should be selected in such a way that the highest priority features have to be developed and delivered early so that an early feedback is received from the stake holders. If the customer is not totally satisfied, the changes can be done in the increments.
- Requirements Management: The changes requested by the customer have to be explicitly managed such that the changes are analyzed before accepting them.
- Use component-based architecture: It is expected that the system architecture consists of manageable components that can be reused, modified, and plugged effectively.

- Model Visually: It is suggested to use visual modeling tools like Unified Modelling Language (UML) for better understanding of the system.
- Maintain Quality: It has to be ensured that the system confirms to the required quality standards.
- Manage change: It is expected that proper Change management and configuration management procedures are in place.

1.7 AGILE DEVELOPMENT PROCESS

Systems across the globe often change rapidly. The business can sustain itself if it can respond to the changing economic situation, market competition, and development of new and emerging systems. This is possible if the software with desired changes can be developed quickly to respond to the competitors. Hence rapid application development is one of the essential critical requirements, and at the same time, the rapid delivery of the software should not compromise its quality.

As businesses evolve, it is impossible to have a complete set of requirements. Furthermore, as there is no clarity, the requirements may change because the customer needs to figure out how the system is foreseen as the actual requirements are unclear.

1.7.1 Plan Driven Models

In the late 1990s, the software development models had issues when the clients wanted to add a new feature or modify an existing feature to the system during its development. Though changes were incorporated, they resulted in increased costs, scope changes, and delays in the delivery of the product. Earlier, these delays were accepted. Organizations will fall behind in the competition due to the dynamics of the market and consumers if the changes requested are not implemented appropriately.

The planned models. like the waterfall model, involve realization of series of steps in a linear order, as depicted in figure 1.17.

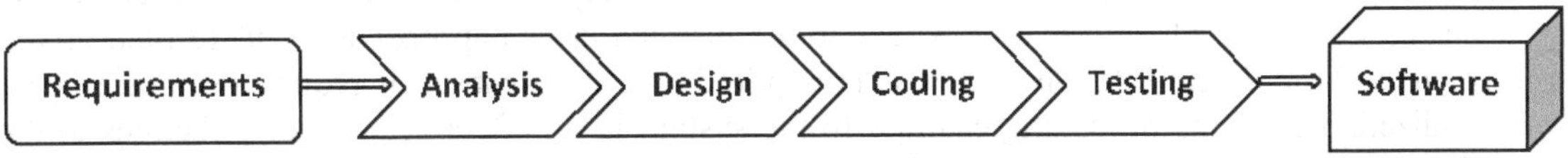

Fig. 1.17: Plan-Driven Model

The plan-driven models are not suitable for small and medium-sized projects. In the planned model, the requirements engineering process is done comprehensively before realizing the system. Detailed specification and documentation are required, and any changes to the system needs specification and documentation to be changed. Such models are suitable for large projects and safety-critical systems.

The drawbacks of the planned-driven model are as follows:

- Changes are difficult to manage
- Less focus on end-user or client needs.
- The effort required to test the system is high.
- Overtime and over budget.

1.7.2 Agile Model

Agile defines a set of principles used in software development that enables faster delivery and early response to changes desired by the customer. Agile refers to a set of methods and practices that focuses on iterative and incremental development. Each iteration in the agile process (fig 1.18) helps develop a piece of the product called increment that can be tested, deployed, and changes to the same may be requested.

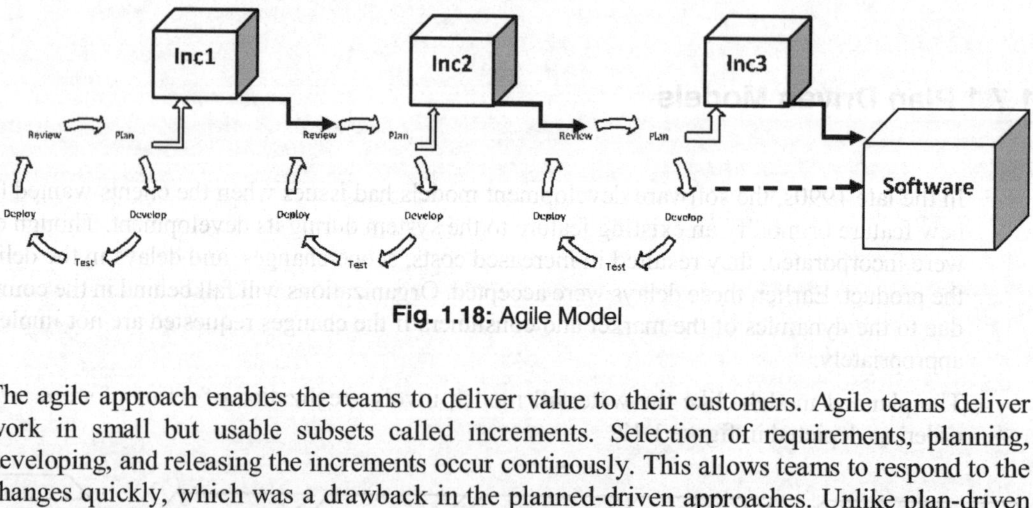

Fig. 1.18: Agile Model

The agile approach enables the teams to deliver value to their customers. Agile teams deliver work in small but usable subsets called increments. Selection of requirements, planning, developing, and releasing the increments occur continously. This allows teams to respond to the changes quickly, which was a drawback in the planned-driven approaches. Unlike plan-driven models, little documentation at a time is required as only a subset of requirements are being realized. This helps in making changes to the system in an effective way, and changes to the documentation are also minimal. The documentation is built incrementally during the agile process. The agile process further allows customer collaboration. During the collaboration, feedback is taken from the customer, which helps manage the changes to the increments. Unlike the planned-driven models, the agile approach will not have a rigid plan. There can be flexibility in planning the scenarios based on the evolving requirements, changes, and priority of the requirements being realized.

The advantages of the Agile process are as follows:

- It helps in seamless interaction between the client and the project team.
- It enables improved transparency to clients in every phase of the project.
- The delivery of each increment's outcome is predictable and can sometimes be earlier than expected as it is clear to understand the pieces of the system.
- The project's cost is predictable and follows a rigid schedule because of improved customer interactions. As we progress, the requirements of the client are better understood.
- Customers can prioritize the system's features, allowing the team to ensure the maximum project value. By assessing customers' prorities, the agile team can deliver expected functionalities.
- The team can deliver cutomer value by focusing on the user's needs.

1.7.3 Agile Principles

The Principles (Agile Manifesto) that have to be followed to realize an Agile model are as follows:

- Customer Satisfaction: Customer satisfaction needs to strive through early and quick delivery of increments. If the part of the system can be delivered to the customer quickly, it increases customer satisfaction.
- Change requests: Change need to be addressed even during the late development process. There should be flexibility in design so that the changes can be accepted at any time in the future.
- Deliver Frequently: Ensure that the software is delivered regularly in smaller modules and continuously integrated so that the final artifact results in a quality product. This should be done regularly so that the customers use the software and give feedback at regular intervals.
- Collaboration. Developers and businesses need to work together throughout the project. Involving customer, developers and team members, leads to better collaboration and helps in receiving continuous feedback from all the stake holders, and getting all together will increase the business values. This also makes the process more transparent. The interactions within the teams should increase for greater understanding and clarity.
- Working Software. The deliverable must be completed regularly so that the customer can give feedback, which not only helps improve the current build but also helps in knowing the customer's perspective for the further pieces of software which will be released in time to come.
- Good design: Agility can be improved by focusing on better design. Detailed design of small working pieces will be better and quicker than designing the entire system at once. Further, it helps in developing pluggable components.
- Simplicity: The effort required on unimportant or non-value activities has to be eliminated. Only the desired activities need to be included.

1.7.4 Agile Methodologies

Agile practices can be demonstrated by following various agile methodologies. This includes XP (Extreme Programming), SCRUM, LEAN, Kanban, etc. In this chapter, the SCRUM framework will be discussed in detail.

SCRUM is a framework that was first introduced in 1986 that helps team members with diverse expertise to work together to achieve a common goal. In SCRUM team, one can learn from experience and brainstorming that helps to enjoy success, perform necessary corrections in case of failures, and learn from mistakes. In the SCRUM, the work is split into several iterations called sprints. Each member in the sprint team has a role to play. They are about 5 to 8 members in a sprint team. The sprint team is a cross-functional team consisting of members with diverse expertise. This not only increases productivity but also enhances the motivation of the team. The advantage of the SCRUM is that the team can efficiently provide project deliverables within the estimated budget and planned schedule. Each sprint is divided into several tasks to keep track of the sprint backlog.

There are various roles of a SCRUM team. This includes the Product Owner, Scrum Master and the Scrum Team.

- The *Product owner* is primarily responsible for maximizing the benefits by determining the product features, prioritizing into a list what needs to be focused on for the next sprint, and constantly reprioritizing and refining it. A product owner has to assess the customer's requirements, identify the features and prioritize the same.
- *Scrum Master* helps teams learn and apply scrum to obtain business value. He/She helps remove impediments, protects them from interference, and helps the team to adopt agile practices. Whenever there are impediments, the scrum master should help teams to solve and move ahead. His focus is to see the scrum team works. There should be a good handshake with the product owner and scrum master.
- *Scrum Team* is a collection of all individuals working together to deliver the stakeholders requirements. They contribute at the individual level. This team should clearly understand the deliverables which they have to deliver.

The various artifacts of Scrum are as follows:

- Product Backlog: It consists of a list of features, changes to be made to the existing features, bug fixes, changes to infrastructure, and other activities that the team needs to deliver.

- Sprint Backlog: The backlog contains the tasks the team aims to complete to realize a lot of work. This piece of software is delivered by the team in a short period of iteration, typically 2-4 weeks. Each sprint can be divided into several tasks.

- Product increment: The part of a system that is ready to use at the end of a sprint is an increment. As the sprints evolve over time, system's functionalities have to be integrated incrementally so that the system is working correctly. The combination of all completed sprints is a product increment. The customer can start using the product increment and give feedback for changes, if any.

The Scrum Framework is specified in figure 1.19.

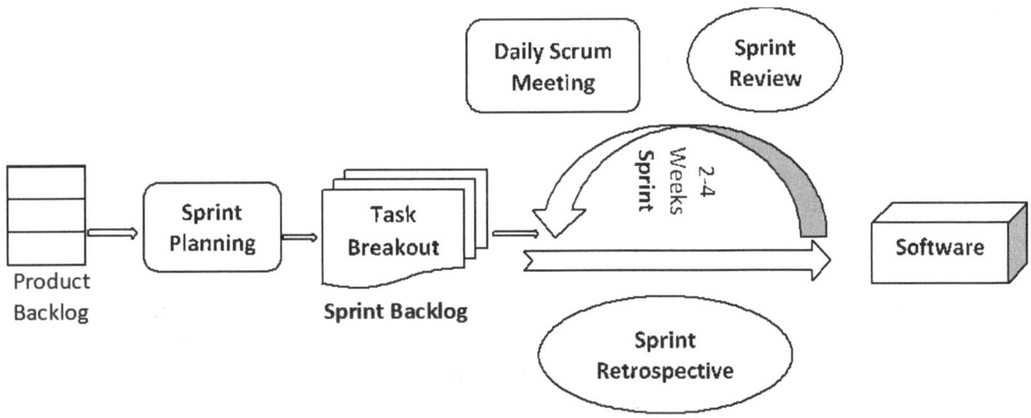

Fig. 1.19: SCRUM Framework

The product owner collects the requirements from the customer and lists the features needed to realize the system. These features of the system are listed in a product backlog. The product owner and the Sprint team prioritize the requirements based customer's needs. The Sprint planning phase defines what can be delivered in the sprint. The features added to the product backlog are commonly referred as a Story.

A story is the basic unit of work in the Agile framework. A user story gives a general description of the software feature from the perspective of stakeholder or a customer. The general form of a story is as follows

As a <*type of user*> **I want to** <*perform some task*> **so that I can** <*achieve some goal*>

Eg. As a *Consumer* I want to *pay bill* so that I can *settle my bills on time*

Each story is divided into several tasks. These tasks have to be designed and implemented to complete a sprint. Test cases are planned (Acceptance test criteria) for each task so that test cases can be executed after its implementation. The list of tasks for each sprint is maintained in Sprint Backlog. Typically a sprint is realized in 2-4 weeks of time. At the end of each day, the sprint team meets for short time to provide updates about the work done, their following plans and any issues they encountered. This is known as daily scrum or stand-up meeting.

In the above example, the *pay bill* story can be divided into several tasks. This includes (a) Design and development of a pay bill page or form with specific validations, (b) Search for the bill, (c) payment options (d) Generate acknowledgement. These tasks are stored in a sprint backlog. For each task, test cases are planned so that functionality can be tested once it is realized.

Once the sprint is completed, it is tested and released. The customer starts using the increment and constantly gives feedback to the customer. Accordingly, the changes are made to the system. In sprint review meeting, the scrum team assesses what was achieved in the sprint. A sprint retrospective meeting is conducted before the next sprint starts but after the completion of the current sprint review. Sprint restrospective meeting is used to assess what went well and what can be improved in the coming sprints.

1.7.5 Banking Scenario

Consider the automation of the Personal Banking System (PBS). The product owner collects the requirements for the realization of PBS. These features are stored in a Product Backlog. Assume that the Product Backlog includes the following features:

- Open Account
- Perform transactions
- Loan Processing

Assume that in the sprint planning meeting, the product owner and sprint team prioritize the stories in the following order: Open Account, Perform transactions, and Loan Processing. Consider the first sprint, "Open Account." The different tasks for the "Open Account" functionality are as follows

- Develop a user interface seeking personal information along with necessary validations
- Create a database to store the personal information
- Provide options for upload of the necessary documents.
- Develop the KYC (Know Your Customer) process

The above tasks constitute the sprint backlog. Before realizing each of these tasks, the test Cases (Acceptance test criteria) are generated for each of these tasks.

- Check whether the Customer is able to access the Account Opening form
- Check whether the Customer is prompted to enter the personal information
- Check whether necessary validations are done
- Check whether the data is stored in the database
- Check whether the customer can upload the necessary documents
- Check whether KYC is completed and the Customer receives OTP
- Check whether the OTP validation is completed and the customer is given the necessary acknowledgement

Similarly, there will be a sprint backlog for each of the stories listed in the product backlog. Each of the tasks listed in the sprint backlog is implemented and then tested. Once all tasks are completed, the piece of the software is ready for the customer to use and give feedback. Once the second story is ready for release, the two increments are integrated to test the functionality of both increments together. This helps in achieving seamless integration of various increments.

UNIT SUMMARY

- ***Software Engineering Prelimaries***
    - *Software*
    - *Software Engineering Vs Systems Engineering*
    - *4P's of Software Development*
    - *Roles, activity and artifacts*

- ***Challenges in Software Development***

- ***Software Quality Attributes***

- **Software Development**
    - *Software Process*
    - *Software Development Activities*

- **Generic Development Process**
    - *Waterfall Model*
    - *Component based software development*

- **Iterative Development Process**
    - *Evolutionary Model*
    - *Incremental Development Model*
    - *Spiral Model*
    - *Unified Process Model*
    - *Best Practices*

- **Agile Development Process**
    - *Planned-Driven Model*
    - *Agile Model*
    - *Agile Principles*
    - *Agile Methodologies*
    - *SCRUM framework*

EXERCISES

Multiple Choice Questions

1.1 The Software assets generally include
(a) Software (b) Operational instructions (c) Documentation (d) All of the above

1.2 Software development activities that are carried out after the deployment of the software is
(a) Software Design (b) Coding (c) Software Maintenance (d) Software Testing

1.3 A System is said to be_________ if it does not produce any dangerous or costly failures
(a) Reliable (b) Compatibe (c) Interoperable (d) Maintainable

1.4 The ability of the system to make use of optimal resources is its _________
(a) Efficiency (b) Reliability (c) Maintainablility (d) redundancy

1.5 The ability of a system to exchange services or data with other systems is known as
(a) Reliability (b) Interoperability (c) Compatibility (d) Reusability

1.6 Software maintenance, which deals with modification to the existing functionality or addition of new feature(s) is
(a) Corrective maintenance (b) Adaptive maintenance
(c) Perfective maintenance (d) Predictive maintenance

1.7 In one of the following process models, each phase is frozen before moving to the next development phase
(a) Incremental Model (b) Prototype Model (c) Waterfall Model (d) Spiral Model

1.8 Risk management is implemented in one of the following process models
(a) Waterfall Model (b) Spiral Model
(c) Incremental Model (d) Unified Process Model

1.9 The number of phases in the unified process model is
(a) 5 (b) 2 (c) 3 (d) 4

1.10 The goal of testing is to
(a) Correct programs (b) Fail programs (c) Design programs (d) Find errors

Answers of Multiple Choice Questions
1.1 (d), 1.2(c), 1.3(a), 1.4(a), 1.5(b), 1.6(c), 1.7(c), 1.8 (b), 1.9(d), 1.10 (d)

Short and Long Answer Type Questions

1.1 Why operational requirements and Documentation is needed for a Software
1.2 Differentiate between the user and the system manual.
1.3 Why do we need a System manual? Give reasons
1.4 Differentiate between software and systems engineering
1.5 What is the need for engineering software?
1.6 List the issues you faced while developing a program or a software. Give reasons
1.7 Describe the quality characteristics of a Software
1.8 List and explain the artifacts of the requirements engineering process
1.9 What is debugging
1.10 What is the goal of testing
1.11 What are the advantages and disadvantages of the waterfall model
1.12 Specify the necessary pre-requisites required to use a Component-Based Software Development Process
1.13 Differentiate between Exploratory Development and Throwaway Prototyping
1.14 List the advantages and disadvantages of Component-Based Software Development
1.15 When the unified process model uses the good features of all process models, what is the need for other process models? Give justification
1.16 List the best practices of Unified Process
1.17 What is a Unified process? What are the milestones of each phase
1.18 Differentiat between Plan driven and agile process model
1.19 Explain the agile principles with the justification of each of these principles.
1.20 Explain the SCRUM methodology.
1.21 Explain when the Agile methodology can fail?

PRACTICAL

1.1 Download any open-source software. Lists its operational requirements and explore the user and system manual.

1.2 Identify various processes in the following systems and identify roles, activities, and artifacts. Draw a process diagram.
(a) Banking System (b) Railway reservation System (c) Online Shopping System

1.3 Identify product backlog, sprint backlog for each sprint, tasks of each sprints and test cases of each sprints to develop (a) Railway reservation System (b) Online Shopping System

KNOW MORE

A Program consists of a set of instructions. The software includes a set of programs along with documentation and operational guidelines. The software which is developed without following standard practices may have many bugs, and will be harder to maintain. Hence a systematic approach for the program or software development is needed.

A software process consists of a set of proven development activities. These activities need to be adopted for the development of software. The first step is the Requirements engineering process. The developer has to understand the needs of customers, or the developer has to understand the system being used by the customer. Several techniques are used for collecting requirements from the customer. This includes Interviews, Questionnaires, Record reviews, observations etc

The developer may directly talk to the customer to understand the requirements. This can be through face-to-face interaction termed as Interviews. If there are many customers, interviews may not be the appropriate technique. In such a case, a questionnaire can be prepared and distributed to customers to collect the requirements. Either of these techniques is insufficient to collect the requirements. For completeness additional techniques like record reviews and observations are used. In record reviews, the developer inspects the records which customers use in its operations. In the observation technique, the developer observes the activities done by the customer. The requirements collected can be classified as functional and non-functional requirements. The functional requirements depict the core functionalities of the system. Additionally, the non-functional requirements like security, readability, reliability, etc need to be considered as per the need.

After understanding the requirements correctly, a plan has to be prepared such that the software is developed within the estimated time and budget. A graphical representation of the system helps better understand the system. Hence a software model is needed. The structure of the software system has to be decided at this stage. The design of a system typically includes its components or elements and the association between them. This is referred to as software architecture.

A complex system can be better understood if it can be divided into sub-systems called modules. These modules can be further divided into sub-modules until the functional component can be properly designed and developed. Once the design is ready, it is converted to a target programming language. The code is developed based on the design produced. While developing the system, the non-functional characteristics need to be considered. For example, if one has to satisfy reusability, the code has to be developed in such a way that the functional units can be reused later.

Once the coding is completed, each function or module is tested for bugs. Testing aims to find bugs in the system. Once individual units are tested successfully, the functional units are integrated and tested. Later the system is again tested with the actual inputs taken from the customer. The system is then deployed and tested. Once the system is built successfully, the user documentation and training process has to be realized. After delivery of the software product, the customer may request modifications to the system. There the software maintenance process begins.

REFERENCES AND SUGGESTED READINGS

- Sommerville, I. (2016) Software Engineering. 10th Edition, Pearson Education Limited, Boston

- Roger S. Pressman (2010) Software Engineering: A Practitioner's Approach, McGraw-Hill

- Rajib Mall (2018), Fundamentals of Software Engineering, 5th Edition, PHI Learning Private Limited.

- Pankaj Jalote (2010), Software Engineering: A Precise Approach, Wiley-India

- Boehm-1988Conny, CC BY-SA 3.0 <http://creativecommons.org/licenses/by-sa/3.0/>, via Wikimedia Commons

Dynamic QR Code for Further Reading

2 Requirements Engineering

UNIT SPECIFICS

Through this unit we have discussed the following aspects:

- *Requirements engineering and its need;*
- *Requirements Taxonomy;*
- *Requirements elicitation techniques;*
- *Requirements Analysis;*
- *Requirements Specification;*
- *Requirmenets Validation;*

The practical applications of the topics are discussed for generating further curiosity and creativity as well as improving problem solving capacity.

Besides giving multiple choice questions as well as questions of short and long answer types marked in two categories following lower and higher order of Bloom's taxonomy, assignments, a list of references and suggested readings are given in the unit so that one can go through them for practice. It is important to note that for getting more information on various topics of interest some QR codes have been provided in different sections which can be scanned for relevant supportive knowledge.

After the related practical, based on the content, there is a "Know More" section. This section has been carefully designed so that the supplementary information provided in this part becomes beneficial for the users of the book. This section mainly highlights the initial activity, examples of some interesting facts, analogy, history of the development of the subject focusing the salient observations and finding, timelines starting from the development of the concerned topics up to the recent time, applications of the subject matter for our day-to-day real life or/and industrial applications on variety of aspects, case study related to environmental, sustainability, social and ethical issues whichever applicable, and finally inquisitiveness and curiosity topics of the unit.

RATIONALE

The first step towards developing software systems is to understand the needs or requirements of the customer. One of the reasons for the failure of the software systems is the inability to understand the actual customer's requirements by the developers. Hence, a systematic approach is needed to collect, analyze, specify, and validate the requirements.

The challenge for software developers is gathering all the customer's requirements. A communication gap between customers and developers often leads to misunderstanding the customer's requirements. If there is no clarity, then the system that is developed will not meet customer's expectations, and the effort spent on developing the systems may get wasted.

Once the requirements are collected, it has to be analyzed to remove any anomalies. Furthermore, understanding the requirements can be clear if a model is developed and the specifications are well documented. The requirements engineering process will also help to understand the requirements that evolve over time.

In the requirements engineering process, the system's feasibility is assessed first. Once it is found that the system is feasible enough the requirements collection begins. Several techniques are used to collect the requirements from the customers.

The requirements collected may have several gaps or anomalies. In order to address the problems in the requirements, it is analyzed, modeled and detailed specifications are written. If the requirements are correctly understood and documented, then the design and development will be as per the collected requirements.

This unit helps students to understand the requirements engineering process. This includes feasibility study, requirements elicitation techniques, requirements analysis and modeling, requirements specification and requirements validation.

PRE-REQUISITES

Computer Programming (Diploma Semester-III)

Scripting Languages (Diploma Semester-III)

UNIT OUTCOMES

List of outcomes of this unit is as follows:

U2-O1: Understand the requirements elicitation techniques

U2-O2: Understand the requirements types

U2-O3: Understand object-oriented and structured analysis paradigms.

U2-O4: Document the requirements specification

U2-05: Understand the importance of requirements validation

Unit-2 Outcomes	EXPECTED MAPPING WITH COURSE OUTCOMES (1- Weak Correlation; 2- Medium correlation; 3- Strong Correlation)				
	CO-1	CO-2	CO-3	CO-4	CO-5
U2-O1	2	3	1	1	2
U2-O2	2	3	1	1	2
U2-O3	2	3	1	1	2
U2-O4	2	3	1	1	2
U2-05	2	3	1	1	2

2.1 REQUIREMENTS ELICITATION

The requirements engineering process includes elicitation, analysis, specification, and validation. Once the system's feasibility is assessed, the requirements collection has to begin. The processing of collecting the features or characteristics of the system from its users or customers is known as requirements elicitation or system study. The requirements elicitation aims to understand the system features from the customer. The requirements engineering team interacts with stakeholders to gather the services and features from the stakeholders.

The stakeholders may express requirements in different ways. The requirements engineering team is expected to have the ability to understand the staekholder's needs. Further, as there could be diverse requirements, an individual with experience in customer's domain may can understand the system better.

There can be various ways to collect stakeholder requirements, known as requirements elicitation techniques. This includes Interviews, Surveys, Rccord views, Ethnography, Stories or scenarios, Use cases, etc.

2.1.1 Interviews

The requirements engineering team or the analyst interacts with the stakeholders to understand the features of the system to be developed or of the system currently in use. In these interviews, the requirements are collected from the resoponses given by the stakeholders.

Interviews are generally of two types:

- Structured or closed interviews: The stakeholders answer questions prepared by the requirements engineering team. In structured interviews, responses to pre-defined questions will be collected. Hence it may not be possible to get more insights into the customer's requirements based on the responses to pre-defined questions.

- Unstructured or open interviews: The open interviews do not have any specific agenda. The requirements engineering team can ask questions to the stakeholders based on the interactions. The stakeholders are free to specify the system's features and express any difficulties in the system. However, the requirements engineering team may overlook some of the system's essential features, which otherwise would have been collected using a structured technique.

It is preferred that both structured and unstructured interviews are required for the proper collection of requirements of a system. The requirements engineering team may begin collecting requirements in an unstructured way. However, as the interview process progresses, one of the team members may look into the predefined questions to check whether some critical questions related to requirements collection need to be covered.

The interview is one of the preferred mechanisms for collecting requirements provided the requirements engineering team consists of members who are domain experts. For example, properly studying the banking system will be easier if the team members know the banking domain.

2.1.2 Questionnaire

An interview is a preferred approach to collecting requirements from customers. However, if there are many stakeholders, it will take more time to collect requirements through the interview process. In such a situation, a Questionnaire is used. A questionnaire consists of a set of questions to collect requirements from the stakeholders. The questionnaires generally consist of both closed-ended and open-ended questions.

In close-ended questions, the stakeholders can pick answers from several choices. The user may be asked to select any of the two choices (True or False) or one option from multiple options or may have to select more than one option from the given options. In open-ended questions, the stakeholders can give descriptive responses to express the functionality or constraints of the system.

Though a questionnaire is used when the information has to be gathered from many stakeholders, there could be various issues. This may include problems with understanding a question or response by stakeholders, or in some cases; their responses may be biased.

2.1.3 Record view

Interviews or Questionnaires alone are not sufficient to gain a proper understanding of the system under study. In addition to interviews or questionnaires, other elicitation techniques like record view and ethnography must be used to get insights into the requirements collection.

In record view techniques, the requirements engineering team gathers the data and facts from the records and documents to understand the system. For example, the requirements engineer may view the examination form and grade sheet to automate a result processing system. This helps in understanding the requirements correctly, and if any details are missed during the interaction with the stakeholders, they will be included in this approach.

2.1.4 Ethnography

Each organization has its way of functioning. In this fact-finding approach, the requirements engineering team studies the system by observing and examining the way the system works. In this way, the requirements are collected from the stakeholders. There are instances where the software systems are developed and delivered, but the stakeholders are unsatisfied. One of the reasons is that the requirements needed to take into account the social and organizational factors of the system. Ethnography helps to observe and understand the operational processes that help develop a system per the stakeholder's actual needs.

For example, the general examination process is the same for all the Institutions across the country. However, each academic institutions have their requirements that differ from others. The Ethnography approach helps observe the system's functionality so that the requirements can be adequately understood.

Generally, Interviews or Questionnaires are used to collect the requirements in the first phase. However, more than this will be required; hence other approaches like Record view, Ethnography are used for collecting detailed requirements.

2.2 SOFTWARE REQUIREMENTS

The software requirements indicate the customer's needs that describe the services a system is expected to provide. It also lists the constraints on the system's operations, if any. The process of collecting, analyzing, specifying, documenting, and validating the requirements is called requirements engineering.

Requirements are generally collected for the system that has to be developed from scratch. However, the requirements for modifications of existing systems can also be provided by the customer. This includes the addition of functionalities to the existing system or modifications to the functionalities already implemented.

The major challenge in the requirements engineering process is understanding the customer's requirements. It is generally seen that there is a gap in understanding the requirements the way the customer wants. If the requirements are not properly understood, then each other phase of the software development will be erroneous. This can be addressed by following certain principles. Firstly, there should be a clear separation between various categories of requirements. Secondly, the collected requirements have to be analyzed and modeled to correct the anomalies in the requirements. Thirdly a detailed specification of the requirements is generally required for plan-driven approaches.

2.2.1 User and System Requirements

In the requirements engineering process, the developers realize the services that the customers or clients requested. The user requirements are the need statements expressed by the customer that gives an abstract description of what the system is expected to provide and the constraints of the system. They are generally written in the customers language that describes the system's desired features to be developed.

The system requirements or functional specifications are the detailed description of the system's functionality, services and operational constraints. The system requirements include a structured technical document that details the user requirements. It is generally written for the developers of the system.

Consider the example of the Student Results Processing System.

Users requirements definition:

Generate results of the students at the end of the semester

System requirements specification:

- Students register for the examination.
- The instructor enters the marks of the eligible students before the last date of result processing.
- The system computes the results of each student for the subjects registered and computes the grade.
- Once the results are processed, they can be viewed.
- Accordingly, the customizable reports can be generated.

2.2.2 Functional and Non-functional requirements

System requirements are generally classified into functional and non-functional requirements. The functional requirements specify the features or services expected by the users or clients of the system. Thus a system can be viewed as a set of functions {fi}.

Each function takes desired input(s) from the input set I and transforms it into an output.

$f: I \rightarrow O$ indicates function f that transforms an input I_i from the input domain I to a value O_j in the output domain O.

In addition to the input and output, the functionalities may also have pre-conditions. The pre-conditions specify the conditions that have to be satisfied before executing a particular function.

The functional requirements of the system requirements specification specified in section 2.2.1 are as follows:

Function	**Input**	**Output**	**Pre-condition**
Examination Registration	Student fills examination form	Acknowledgement	Should be a valid student.
Evaluate student	Instructor enters mars	Result computed	Students should have appeared for examination
Process Results	Results of individual courses	Final grade sheet	All subjects marks has to be entered.

Fig. 2.1: Functional requirements

Additionally, there will be a function called "Generate report" which takes a user query and generates the corresponding reports. It could display the list of students who have secured specific grades, list of students who could not pass a course etc. The pre-condition for the "Generate report" function is that the result processing functionality is realized.

The Non-functional requirements do not directly deal with the services or functionalities of the system. However, it represents specific constraints of the system. They constitute quality characteristics of the system and can vary from one application to another. This includes reliability, maintainability, portability, reusability, security, performance, usability etc.

Performance: The ability of the system to fulfill the desired performance requirements. For example, it is desired that the system should be able to allow 10,000 students to register for examinations at a time without any delay. The examination registration is a functional requirement. However, the same functionality is expected to execute correctly when 10,000 students access the system.

Reliability: The ability of the system to avoid dangerous or costly failures. For example, on the last day of the examination registration, if the system fails and can't recover quickly, it may lead to chaos, thus making it unreliable. Hence there is a need to plan for recovering the system within a short period in case of severe failures.

Portability: The ability of the system to work in other environments. For example, suppose the system is developed in one operating environment. In that case, it should be able to work on other environments (on different hardware or software environments) with minimal changes.

Usability: The ability of the system to provide its users perform tasks efficiently without any difficulty. For example, a user with any background should be able to use an application easily.

Security: The system's ability to ensure that it is protected against any unauthorized access or attacks. Only authorized users must be allowed to use the system. It is to be ensured that the data is protected against any attacks.

Maintainability: The ability of the system to accept the changes. Whenever changes or modifications are required to the system, it should be able to incorporate the same without many changes to the existing functionalities.

2.3 REQUIREMENTS ANALYSIS & SPECIFICATION

The requirements are collected using fact-finding techniques. However, the requirements can not be adequately understood and may result in developing a system that the customer may not accept. In order to better understand the system, it has to be modeled, i.e., a blueprint or a pictorial representation of the requirements might help in adequately understanding the same.

Secondly, the requirements collected may contain several anomalies. This includes ambiguities, incompleteness, and inconsistencies. These anomalies need to be identified and rectified.

The requirements analysis aims to properly understand the requirements so that there is no inconsistency, incompleteness, or ambiguity.

- Ambiguity: When several interpretations of the same requirements can be made, it is ambiguous. In the result processing system example, if a student is not performing well in formative assessments, the mentors need to be informed about the same. In this requirement, "Student not performing" cannot be quantified as it is ambiguous. The requirements engineering team needs to address such ambiguity in consultation with the stakeholders.

- Inconsistency: If the requirements collected contradict each other, they are said to be inconsistent. This may happen if one stakeholder specifies certain features of the system and other stakeholders contradict the same or the same stakeholders contradict the given requirements at different intervals. For example, one staff member in the Academic section says that a student can be promoted if there are no more than 50% of backlogs, and the other staff says one can carry four backlogs. If there are six courses in a semester, then the given requirement regarding the promotion contradicts.

- Incompleteness: The requirement is incomplete if the customer or stakeholder cannot anticipate certain system features and may realize them later. However, the requirements engineering team or an analyst can suggest to the customer the incomplete requirements in the given system. For example, an academic institution enters the grades of students based on the marks secured. However, the policy of grading may differ from one institution to another. As a result, students may not get uniform grades when they take courses from other institutions.

These anomalies have to be addressed by the requirements engineering team or an analyst in consultation with stakeholders.

In order to properly understand the system, it is better to model it. There are broadly two paradigms for analyzing a system: Object Oriented Analysis and Structured System Analysis.

Object-oriented modeling is an approach to writing a blueprint of the application that is used to develop object-oriented systems. Unified Modeling Language (UML) is used to write software blueprints. UML is a language that is used for visualizing the system. Additionally, detailed specifications are to be provided for each element in UML, and finally, it is translated into implementation. The target programming language used in this approach is an object-oriented programming language. The application is being developed using object-oriented programming constructs.

Structured system modeling helps develop a blueprint of the application in terms of processes in the system. The target programming language in this paradigm is structured.

2.3.1 Object Oriented Analysis

Object oriented analysis is an approach to tranform the requirements into an object-oriented model. The significant artifacts of the object-oriented analysis phase are the use case model and identification of Analysis Classes. A use case model specifies the functionality of the system.

The following steps are to be followed for modeling a use case

- **Identify Actors**
  The first step in use case modeling is to identify actors in the system. An actor is an entity that interacts with the system or its functionalities and is generally outside the boundary of the system. It can be a human being, a hardware device, or a legacy system. An Actor can be visually represented as follows:

Fig. 2.2: Actor

- **Identify the behavior of each actor (use case)**
  For each actor, identify its behavior which is a use case. A use case is a set of sequence of actions whose outcome is given back to its actor. The functional requirements are captured in use cases. An use case is visually represented as an ellipse.

Fig. 2.3: Use case

- **Draw Preliminary use case diagram**

  A use case diagram contains actors, use cases, and relationships. The relationship between an actor and a use case is an Association. Association is a structural relationship between two things. An Association can be unidirectional or bi-directional. An Association is represented by a thick single line between two things.

Association	
Uni-directional association	

Fig. 2.4: Association

A use case diagram is of the following form.

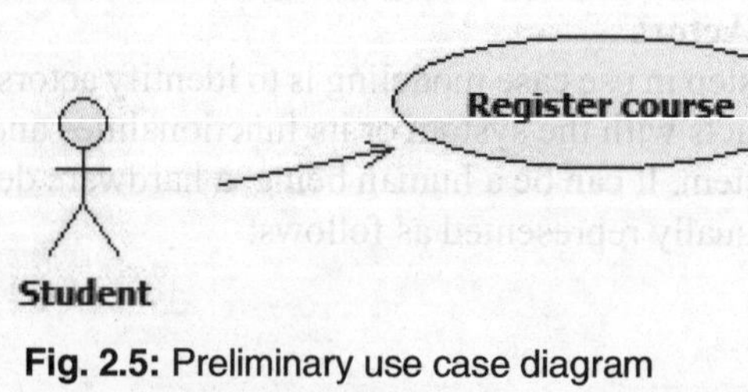

Fig. 2.5: Preliminary use case diagram

- **Refine use case diagram**

The use case diagram can be refined by visualizing relationships between use cases. There might be dependencies between use cases. If a particular functional requirement must be executed before the other functionality begins, then it is visualized using dependency relationship.
If the change in specification of one thing reflects the other thing, then it is a dependency relationship which is represented using dotted arrow ....>

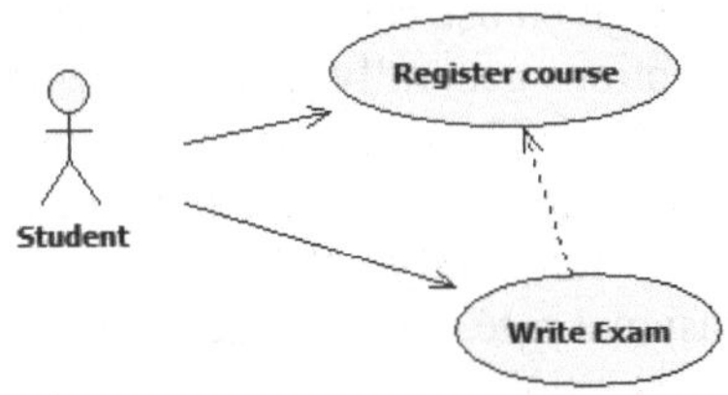

Fig. 2.6: Refined use case diagram

The above use case diagram shows that the "Write Exam" use case is dependent on "Register Course" use case. A student can write an exam only if the registration for the course is completed.

- **Write use case specification**

A use case diagram alone is insufficient to understand the requirements. In order to ensure that requirements are complete, consistent and unambiguous, it is necessary to write a detailed specification.
The general template for use case specification is given in the figure 2.7.

Use Case ID:			
Use Case Name:			
Created By:		Last Updated By:	
Date Created:		Date Last Updated:	
Actors:			
Description:			
Preconditions:			
Post conditions:			
Normal Flow:			
Alternate Flows:			
Exceptions:			
Priority:			
Frequency of Use:			
Business Rules:			
Assumptions:			

Fig. 2.7: Use case Specification template

The first part of the above figure specifies the general characteristics of the Use case specification. This includes the use case name, name of the person who wrote the specification, date of creation, and modification. Then the detailed use case specification is given. Actors specify the entities which interact with various functionalities of the system which are captured in the use case. A short description of the use case is given in the Description section. The pre-condition specifies the conditions that must be satisifed before executing the function. The postconditions indicate the outcome of the realization of a given specification.

The primary or Normal flow and Alternate flows specify the description of the sequence of activities of a given use case. Each of these activities indicates an activity or an action state. The exceptions generally specify the condition which is realized when the use case goal is not achieved. There can be several use cases in a system. However, based on its importance, the priority high, medium or low can be specified. Frequency of use indicates how frequently the actors will use the use case. It may be frequent/occasional/rare. The business rules for the implementation of the use case is specified in this section. The assumptions and dependencies, if any, in implementing this use case are given.

- **Identify Analysis Classes**

  The analysis classes represent the abstract classes of the system. This is the first step for moving to design. In this step, the Classes are identified. This generally includes only class names. A class is the description of objects or a set of objects that share the same features and behavior. A class is generally represented pictorially as a three-compartment rectangle.

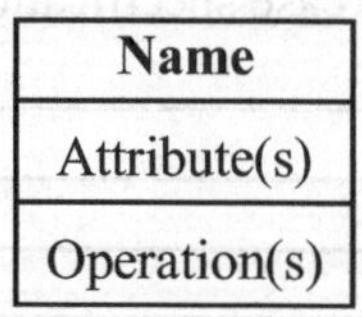

Fig. 2.8: Class representation

Classes are identified from requirements statements generally using two methods viz. Noun Convention and CRC (Class, Responsibility, Collaboration) methods.

First all the nouns are identified and listed. In the second step, redundant nouns (if any) are removed. For example, Student and Candidate are the classes identified in the first step. However, it is redundant as both refer to the same thing. One of them has to be discarded. In the third step, any vague nouns representing classes that are irrelevant to the system's domain are removed. Finally, if any of the characteristics or properties of a class are identified as nouns, they are discarded and included as an attribute of a particular class.

In CRC (Class Responsibility Collaboration) method, the classes are identified as nouns. Furthermore, verbs are extracted from the requirements. The verbs may represent responsibility or collaboration. Responsibility indicates the behavior that will be realized as an operation or a method of a class, whereas collaboration refers to the methods that specify the association between various classes. A CRC card is equivalent to a postal card represented in Figure 2.9.

Name	
Responsbility	**Collaboration**

Fig. 2.9: CRC Card

*

2.3.2 Case Study: Object Oriented Analysis

The Indian Bank offers the following basic operations to its savings account holders: Deposit, Withdrawal &Transfer. The bank teller performs these operations on behalf of the customer. The teller verifies the account number, and if the account number is valid, s/he validates the signature of the customer and performs a deposit or withdrawal operation. For withdrawal operation, the teller additionally checks amount availability. Similarly, for transfer operation, the teller verifies both account numbers and checks for the availability of the amount in the source account.

As the above scenario describes banking operations in an offline or personal mode, the teller acts as an actor on behalf of the customer. The use case diagram for the above scenario is given in Figure 2.10

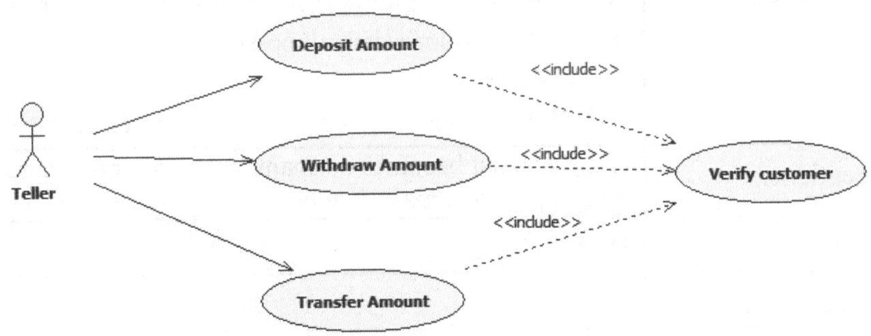

Fig. 2.10: Use Case diagram for banking scenario

Deposit Amount, Withdraw Amount, and Transfer Amount are primary use cases. Verify customer is required before realizing the primary use cases. Hence there is a dependency relationship between such use cases, and verifying customer becomes the pre-condition for the other use cases of the system. In Unified modeling, stereotypes are used to provide additional meaning to the UML constructs. In the use case model, the most common stereotypes used are include and extends. Include relationship is a dependency relationship where the use case (to which the dependency arrow is pointed) is mandatory and part of base case use. In Figure 2.10, verify customer is a mandatory use case and is a part of the Transfer Amount use case, i.e, the transfer amount use case cant proceed with its execution till the verify customer is realized. Similarly, exclude is a dependency relationship where use case is optional and may or may not be part of the base use case.

The next step in use case modeling is to write specifications of the use case model, which is required to visualize the system.

Use Case ID:	Bank001
Use Case Name:	Deposit Amount
Actors:	Teller
Description:	This use case is used by teller on behalf of customer to deposit amount into the account
Preconditions:	The user must be a valid customer of the bank
Post conditions:	Amount is successfully deposited in the account
Normal Flow:	1.1 Verify account number (A-1) 1.2 Verify privileges of the customer (A-2) 1.3 Enter amount (A-3) 1.4 Acknowledge.
Alternative Flows:	A-1: If the account number is invalid, terminate the use case A-2: If the customer doesn't possess valid privileges, terminate the use case. A-3: If the amount entered is improper, re-enter the amount
Exceptions:	If the account becomes dormant, necessary procedures are to be completed to make it active.
Priority:	High
Frequency of Use:	Frequently
Business Rules:	Teller, after verifying the account number, verifies the signature manually
Assumptions:	It is assumed that the customer details are available in the system.

Fig. 2.11: Use case specification for Deposit Amount

Analysis classes identified (Noun Convention): Customer, Account (Account number, Amount)

Refinement of classes through Domain Analysis:

Customer (Id, Name, Address, Contact number, Privileges)

Account (Account number, Amount)

Transaction (Account number, Transaction ID, Type, Amount)

Use Case ID:	Bank002
Use Case Name:	Withdraw Amount
Actors:	Teller
Description:	This use case is used by the teller on behalf of a customer to withdraw the amount from the account
Preconditions:	The user must be a valid customer of the bank.
Post conditions:	Amount is successfully withdrawn from the account or a message is displayed
Normal Flow:	2.1 Verify account number (A-1) 2.2 Verify privileges of the customer (A-2) 2.3 Verify amount (A-3) 2.4 Update account.
Alternative Flows:	A-1: If the customer number is invalid, terminate the use case A-2: If the customer doesn't possess valid privileges, terminate the use case. A-3: If the amount entered is improper or if the minimum balance is not maintained, terminate the use case or re-enter the amount
Exceptions:	If the amount is not available in the account, the customer may still get a certain amount (Overdraft)
Priority:	High
Frequency of Use:	Frequently
Business Rules:	Teller, after verifying the account number, verifies the signature manually Checks the balance amount in the account
Assumptions:	It is assumed that the customer details are available.

Fig. 2.12: Use case specification for Withdraw Amount

Further Refinement of classes through Domain Analysis:

Customer (Id, Name, Address, Contact number)
Account (Account number, Amount)
Transaction (Account Number, Transaction Id, **Date**, Type, Amount, **Remarks**)

Use Case ID:	Bank003
Use Case Name:	Transfer Amount
Actors:	Teller
Description:	This use case is used by the teller on behalf of customer to transfer amount from one account to another account
Preconditions:	Both accounts should be valid
Post conditions:	Amount is successfully deposited in the target account
Normal Flow:	3.1 Verify the account number of the source account holder (A-1) 3.2 Verify the account number of the target account holder (A-1) 3.3 Verify the privileges of customers (A-2) 3.4 Enter Amount (A-3)
Alternative Flows:	A-1: If the customer number is invalid, terminate the use case A-2: If the customer doesn't possess valid privileges, terminate the use case. A-3: If the amount entered is improper, re-enter the amount
Exceptions:	If the amount is not available in the bank, the customer may still get a certain amount (Overdraft)
Priority:	High
Frequency of Use:	Occasionally
Business Rules:	Teller, after verifying the account numbers, verifies the signature of source account manually Teller also checks the minimum balance in source a/c
Assumptions:	It is assumed that the customer's details are available.

Fig. 2.13: Use case specification for Transfer Amount

Analysis classes identified (Noun Convention): Customer, Account (Account number, Amount)

Refinement of classes through Domain Analysis:

Customer (Id, Name, Address, Contact number)

Account (Account number, Amount)

Transaction (Account number, Transaction Id, Type, Amount)

//Against single TransactionId there can be more than one entry (one for deposit another for withdraw //

2.3.3 Structured System Analysis

Structured system analysis is an approach to transform the requirements into a model that will implement the system using procedural languages. The primary artifacts of the structured system analysis phase are the Data Flow Diagrams (DFD), Process Descriptions, and Data Dictionary. Unlike the object-oriented analysis approach, the structured analysis follows a top-down approach. The system uses a divide-and-conquer strategy where the system is split into several subsystems to reduce the complexity.

- **Data Flow Diagram (DFD)**

  The Data Flow Diagram(DFD) describes the data flow between various system processes. The entire system is initially viewed as a single process, which can be decomposed into various sub-processes. The decomposition is continued till the sub-processes are simple to understand.

  The symbols used to model a DFD are specified in Figure 2.14.

Symbol	Name
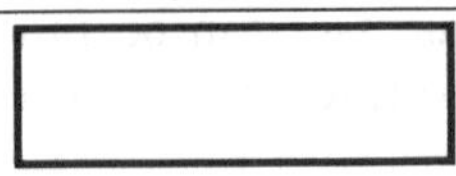	**External Entity**
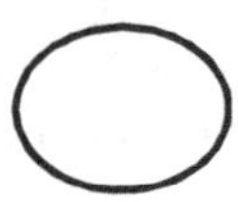	**Process**
	**Data Store**
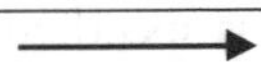	**Data Flow**

Fig. 2.14: Notations used in Data Flow Diagram (DFD)

An External Entity is represented as a rectangle. These entities are external to the system but interact with the system by giving inputs or by extracting the reports. The external entity may also be used to represent any external devices and other applications with which the system may interact. The name of the external entity is specified in the rectangle.

A circle represents a Process. They represent a function that takes inputs from the external entity and returns the results to the same or the other external entity. The process name is specified in the circle. The data store is represented using open-ended rectangle. The data store represents a file, database, or other data storage construct.

Data flow notation is a directed arrow. It is used to show the flow of data in the system. Each of these data flows is labeled to show the data which is flowing in the system. The data may flow from an external entity to the process and vice versa, process to a data store, and vice versa and between the processes of the system.

The basic principles for the construction of a Data Flow Diagram are as follows:

- o The data flow diagram of a system contains a hierarchy of the DFDs. As it follows a top-down approach, the process at the highest abstract level is decomposed into sub-processes as the granularity increases.
- o The first step is to model a context-level data flow diagram. It is also said to be a 0th (zeroth) level DFD. This is the most abstract DFD that represents the entire system as a single process. The external entities that provide input and get output from the system are identified. The data flow is specified using the directed arrows that have appropriate captions.
- o The next step is to model a first-level data flow diagram. That is, the system as a single process will be decomposed into several high-level functional requirements as stated in the software requirements specification document. Each of these requirements represents a process at the first level. Each of the functional requirements can be further exploded in the second level. The first level DFD is also used for system integration where various functionalities can be integrated into a system.
- o Each of the first level DFD processes can be further decomposed into sub-processes. There can be a second level DFD for each of the process identified in the first level.
- o The decomposition can move further to any number of levels. However, the functional decomposition ends when it is observed that the process at the nth level is simple that can be designed and implemented.

- **Process Description**

  Once the DFD is modeled, the specification of each of the processes has to be written. The generic format of the process description is specified in Figure 2.15

Name of the Process	
Input(s)	
Logic	
Output(s)	

Fig. 2.15: Process Description template

Each process in the DFD has a name. The inputs to the process are specified using the data flow arrow, which is given by the external entity. The process tranforms the given input into an expected output. The logic required for this tranformation is written in the Logic section. The output is the outcome of the process, which is returned to the external entity.

- **Data Dictionary**
  Data Dictionary is a file that contains characteristics of the data. In DFD, it is evident that the data flow across external entities, processes, and data stores. The characteristics of these data are stored in the data dictionary.
  The composite data items, if any, are converted into atomic items and entered into the data dictionary. For example, student_details can be a composited data item. It may be divided into Enrollment_no, Name, Course, etc.
  For each of the data items analyzed, its name, generic type, range of values, scope, etc are described.

2.3.4 Case Study: Structured System Analysis

University Library wants to automate the issue and return of books process for its Members. Members can be faculty, student, or Staff. Students can be issued four books at a time, faculty ten books, and staff can take two books at a time. Only the registered members are eligible for the issue of books. The books are issued for a period of 15 days. After that a fine of Rs. 1/= per day is charged. The fine is computed while returning the books. It is assumed that the member's and book's data is available.

The first step is to model a context-level DFD by identifying the system's External entities (source and destination). In the given scenario, Member is the external entity, and it interacts with the system with a request for issuing a book or might return a book. Accordingly, the Member either receives the book or the acknowledgment of receipt. The context level DFD for the given scenario is specified in Figure 2.16

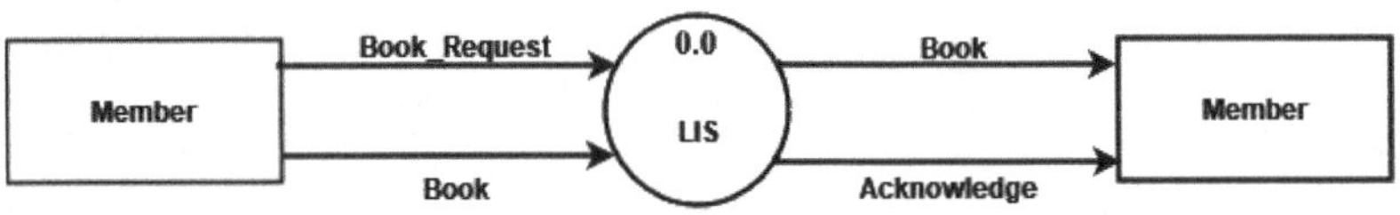

Fig. 2.16: Context Level DFD for LIS

The LIS process is decomposed into subprocesses representing the high-level functional requirements. In the given scenario, the high-level functional requirements are Issue Book and Return Book. The shared data stores may be identified that help in planning for the seamless integration of sub-processes. The first level DFD for the given scenario is given in Fig. 2.17.

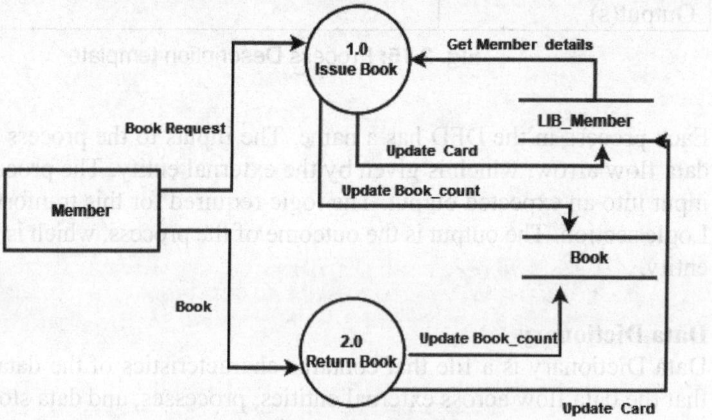

Fig. 2.17: First Level DFD for LIS

Each of the sub-processes can be decomposed into respective DFDs at the second level. As the hierarchy of the level increases, the abstraction decreases, and more details are added. The second level DFDs for Issue Book and Return Book are depicted in Fig 2.18 and Fig 2.19, respectively.

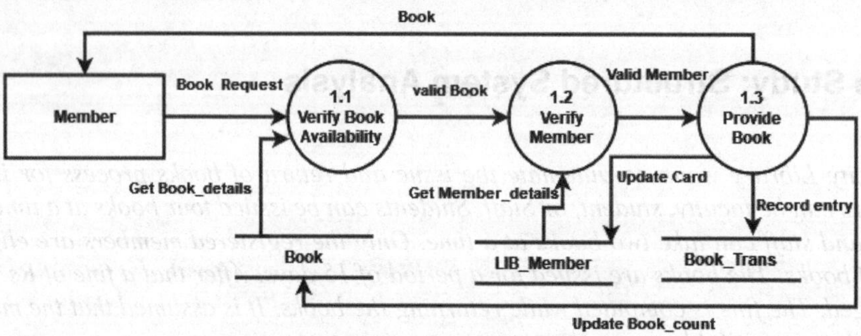

Fig. 2.18: Second Level DFD for Issue Book

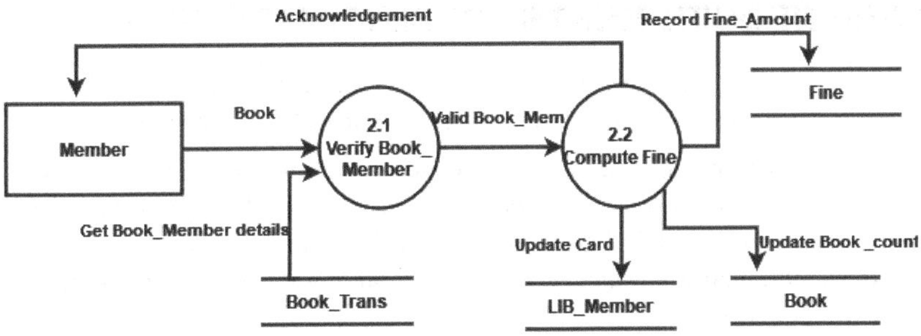

Fig. 2.19: Second Level DFD for Return Book

The specification of each of the functions is a process description. Figure 2.20 gives the process description of a few functions of the given scenario.

Function name	Verify Book Availability
Input	Title, Author, Edition
Output	Book Availability Status
Logic	1. Query Book data store to check whether the book with Title, Author and Edition is available in the library 2. If the book is available, check whether Quantity on hand is not zero 3. If the above two conditions are satisfied, then the search for given book is Successful

Function name	Verify Member
Input	Member Id
Pre- condition	Verify Book Availability function returns true
Output	Member eligibility status
Logic	1. Query Member data store to check whether Member id matches 2. If member is valid, check for the number of books already issued based on type of member 3. If the above two conditions are satisfied, member is eligible for issue of books

Fig. 2.20: Process Decription of few processes of LIS

Similarly, the process description of each of the other processes is documented. The Inputs and outputs from the process description are recorded in the data dictionary, which includes type, range, scope of the datum, etc.

2.4 SOFTWARE REQUIREMENTS SPECIFICATION(SRS)

Software requirements specification is a document that describes a particular product, software, or program that performs a set of functionalities in a specific environment.

SRS helps in documenting the functional and non-functional requirements along with detailed specifications and interfaces. Finally, it helps check whether the system developed meets all the requirements stated in an SRS. The benefit of SRS is that the requirements collected become complete, consistent, unambiguous, verifiable, traceable with further development steps, and can be modified whenever needed.

SRS is generally required for large-scale projects and safety-critical systems that need plan-driven approaches. However, for Small and Medium Size projects that may use an agile approach, a detailed SRS is not required.

According to IEEE recommended practice of Software Requirements Specification, an SRS is divided into four sections. The template for SRS is given below.

1. INTRODUCTION
    - 1.1 Purpose
    - 1.2 Scope
    - 1.3 Definitions, Acronyms, Abbreviations
    - 1.4 References
    - 1.5 Overall Description
2. OVERALL DESCRIPTION
    - 2.1 Product perspective
    - 2.2 Product functions
    - 2.3 User characteristics
    - 2.4 User constraints
    - 2.5 Assumptions & dependencies
    - 2.6 Apportioning requirements
3. SPECIFIC REQUIREMENTS
    - 3.1 Interface requirements
        - 3.1.1 External Interface
        - 3.1.2 Hardware Interface
        - 3.1.3 Software Interface
        - 3.1.4 Communication Interface
    - 3.2 Functional requirements
        - 3.2.1 Use case model / Information Flows
        - 3.2.2 Use Case Specifications/ Process description
        - 3.2.3 Analysis Classes/Data Dictionary
    - 3.3 Performance requirements

3.4 Logical database requirements
3.5 Design Constraints
3.6 Software System attributes
  3.6.1 Reliability
  3.6.2 Availability
  3.6.3 Security
  3.6.4 Maintainability
  3.6.5 Portability

4. SUPPORTING INFORMATION

The first section is the Introduction section of SRS. The purpose specifies the intentions and target audience of the system. It is to be explicitly stated why the system is being developed and who will be using the system. The scope specifies the goals, objectives, and capabilities of the system. Definitions, acronyms, and abbreviations used need to be documented in this section. References used to write SRS is to be included. The overview section specifies the organization of SRS and the description of the remaining parts of SRS.

The overall description section specifies the factors that affect the system and its requirements. The product perspective section specifies whether the product being developed is an independent or a part of a larger system. A block diagram showing system's major parts, interfaces and their connections is preferred. The product functions section lists the primary functional requirements of the system. A list of use cases or processes of the system may be listed with a description. The user characteristics section describes the characteristics of intended users, including educational qualification and technical knowledge required to use the system. The constraints section specifies the conditions that developers need to incorporate. They may also include regulatory policies, standards etc. The assumptions and dependencies upon which the system will be developed have to be stated in this section. Some of the requirements that can be delayed for future can be documented in the apportioning requirements section.

The detailed specifications are given in the "Specific Requirements" section of SRS. The Interface requirements section specifies all the interfaces of the system in detail. The external interface section gives a description of all inputs and outputs of the system. This includes the general characteristics and format of the user interfaces and reports. The hardware interface section specifies the characteristics of the system's hardware components. The software interface section documents the other software's, database's, etc. This includes the name of the the software, version number, source, etc. The communication interface section specifies various interfaces required for communication. This includes LAN, internet, etc.

The functional requirements section details the functionalities listed in the product functions section. If the object-oriented analysis approach is followed, then the use case model, specification of use cases, and analysis classes are listed. In the case of structured analysis, the data flow diagram, process description, and data dictionary has to be specified.

The desired performance requirements of the system can be specified in the performance requirements section. The logical database requirements specify the list of required tables and their access mechanisms. The design constraints specify any hardware limitations, complaince to certain desired standards etc. The system attributes list the desired non-functional characteristics of the system. The supporting information section lists appendixes (if any).

2.5 REQUIREMENTS VALIDATION

Requirements validation assesses whether the requiremenets specified are the same as the stakeholders needs. The requirements validation phase helps minimize the rework that may arise due to the communication gap between the stakeholders and requirements engineers. There may be a need to modify the entire requirement specification document. However, the cost of fixing these anomalies is much lesser compared to being identified later in the development stage.

Several checks are done on the requirements specification document in the requirements validation phase. Some of these checks are also done during the requirements analysis phase. However, in the requirements validation stage, the checks are done on the detailed specification document. This includes checking for consistency, completeness, and unambiguity in the detailed specification. One requirement should not conflict with the other. The requirements document is expected to capture all the desired functionalities of the system. It should also be checked whether the requirements conform to the standards or policies in the problem domain. Several techniques, such as requirements reviews and prototyping are used for requirements validation.

2.5.1 Requirements Review

A team involving all stakeholders will review the requirement specification document in the requirements review. The goal of this review is to identify issues in the requirements specification. The team members review the specification document and check for completeness, consistency, ambiguity, understandability, conformance to standards, traceability etc. The stakeholders are given a check list of the items to be reviewed in the specification document for feedback. Based on the problems reported during the review, the SRS is revised and again submitted for review. This process is repeated till an operational requirement specification document is ready. However this activity need to be planned so that it doesnt effect the product delivery timeline.

2.5.2 Prototyping

In the prototype technique, a working system model is made, which is reviewed by end users of the system. The end users or customers will check whether the model meets their expectations. Accordingly, feedback is given, which is incorporated into the revised prototype. Subsequently, the SRS is updated. Once the operational prototype is accepted, the design phase can start.

UNIT SUMMARY

- ***Requirements Engineering Activities***
- ***Requirements Elicitation Techniques***
  - *Interviews*
  - *Questionnaire*
  - *Record view*
  - *Ethnography*
- ***Software Requirements***
  - *User and System Requirements*
  - *Functional and Non-functional requirements*
- **Requirements Analysis and Specification**
  - *Object Oriented Analysis*
  - *Structured System Analysis*
  - *Case Studies*
- **Software Requirements Specification (SRS)**
- **Requirements Validation**
  - Requirements Review
  - Prototyping

EXERCISES

Multiple Choice Questions

2.1 The requirements elicitation technique that is used when the requirements have to be collected from many stakeholders is

(a) Interview (b) Questionnaire (c) Record view (d) Observation

2.2 The desired quality characteristics of a system is a__________ requirement

(a) Functional (b) System (c) Non-functional (d) Developer

2.3 The functional requirements are captured in

(a) Use case (b) Class (c) CRC (d) System

2.4 The analysis classes can be generated using a CRC Method. CRC Stands for

(a) Class Reasoning Collaboration
(b) Cyclic Redundancy Check
(c) Class Relationship Class
(d) Class Responsibility Collaboration

2.5 If the change in the specification of a use case-A affects the specification of the use case-B, then it is represented using the following relationship

(a) Unidirectional Association (b) Dependency
(c) Bi-directional Association (d) Reusability

2.6 If an application is planned to be developed using a C language, which of the following paradigm is preferred for modeling the system?

(a) OOAD (b) SSAD
(c) Both OOAD & SSAD (d) UML

2.7 In one of the following levels of DFD the entire system is represented as an abstract process

(a) Context Level (b) First Level (c) Second Level (d) Third Level

2.8 The DFD that specifies high-level functional requirements a sub-processes is a _____ level DFD

(a) Context (b) First
(c) Second (d) Third

2.9 One of the following is not a requirements validation technique

(a) Interviews (b) Requirements Review
(c) Prototyping (d) Consistency Checks

2.10 One of the sections of SRS lists a set of requirements that can be considered later

(a) Product Perspective (b) Product Functions
(c) Use Characteristics (d) Apportioning requirements

Answers of Multiple Choice Questions
2.1 (b), 2.2(c), 2.3(a), 2.4(d), 2.5(b), 2.6(b), 2.7(a), 2.8 (b), 2.9(a), 2.10 (d)

Short and Long Answer Type Questions

2.1 What is requirements engineering? What are the various artifacts of requirements engineering

2.2 Explain why ian nterview or questionnaire alone may not be sufficient to collect requirements from stakeholders.

2.3 What are the consequences of not properly understanding the requirements of a stakeholder?

2.4 Differentiate between (i) User and System requirements (ii) Functional and Non-functional requirements.

2.5 When functional requirements represent all desired features of the system, then why the non-function requirements are needed?

2.6 What is object-oriented analysis? Which systems are expected to use this approach

2.7 What is structured system analysis? Which types of systems have to be analyzed using structured system analysis and why

2.8 What is Software Requirements Specification (SRS)? Why is it needed

2.9 Explain why a detailed SRS is not required for the systems following agile methodology

2.10 What is requirements validation? What are the consequences of avoiding requirements validation

2.11 List the tests that are carried out during requirements validation.

2.12 Differentiate between DFD and a flow chart.

PRACTICAL

2.1 Collect requirements from stakeholders for any automation requirement in your institution.

2.2 Identify the target environment in which the application has to be developed and use the appropriate analysis paradigms (Object-oriented or structued) to model the following systems.
(a) Banking System (b) Railway reservation System (c) Online Shopping System

2.3 Develop Software Requirements Specification (SRS) document for (a) Railway reservation System (b) Online Shopping System.

2.4 Model any project using the appropriate analysis paradigms and write the detailed SRS of the same.

KNOW MORE

Requirements engineering is a systematic approach to collecting, analyzing, specifying, and documenting the system's requirements. Once the system is feasible to develop, the requirements collection begins. The mechanism for requirements collection is said to be the requirements elicitation technique. The requirements elicitation techniques are Interviews, Questionnaires, Record view, Observation, etc. The requirements can also be collected using scenarios and even by a requirements document submitted by the customer. This is also referred to as a system study. To better understand the system, it is to be modelled. A model simplifies reality and connects to reality. Through modeling, one can visualize the system. Based on the target environment, the modeling paradigm can be selected. This includes object-oriented and structured paradigms. If it is planned to realize the system in an object-oriented or object-based programming language, object oriented analysis approach is to be followed. If the system is planned to be developed in procedural languages, then the structured analysis approach is used.

The artifacts of the object oriented anlaysis approach include the use case model, use case specification, and Analysis Classes. The use case specification can also be represented visually using an activity diagram. An activity diagram depicts the sequence of activities or actions of a given use case. The activity diagram resembles a flow chart. However, the activity diagrams can also include synchronization of activities. Several scenarios can be visualized using an activity diagram.

The artifacts of structured analysis approach include a data flow diagram, process description, and data dictionary. The object-oriented analysis approach is a bottom-up approach, whereas the structured approach is a top- down approach. In structured analysis, the system is initially viewed as a single process. Later, it is decomposed into hierarchy of processes until we reach simple functions that can be understood and later realized.

Apart from the functional requirements, the system's desired quality characteristics must be defined. Each system has its requirement of quality. These quality parameters have to be tested after testing the system's functionality

In order to ensure that the requirements are complete, consistent or unambiguous, it is required to write software requirements specification, which has to be validated. There are several requirements validation techniques to verify that the requirements collected are as per the customer's needs. Several techniques are used for requirements validation. This includes requirements review and prototyping.

The test cases can be generated from the artifacts of the analysis and from the specification document.

REFERENCES AND SUGGESTED READINGS

- Sommerville, I. (2016) Software Engineering. 10th Edition, Pearson Education Limited, Boston
- Roger S. Pressman (2010) Software Engineering: A Practitioner's Approach, McGraw-Hill
- Rajib Mall (2018), Fundamentals of Software Engineering, 5th Edition, PHI Learning Private Limited.
- Pankaj Jalote (2010), Software Engineering: A Precise Approach, Wiley-India
- Grady Booch, James Rumbaugh, Ivar Jacobson (2017), The Unified Modeling Language User Guide, 2nd Edition, Pearson India Education Services Pvt. Ltd.
- IEEE Recommended Practice for Software Requirements Specifications (830-1993/1998)

Dynamic QR Code for Further Reading

3 Software Design

UNIT SPECIFICS

This unit discusses the following aspects:

- *Design Concepts;*
- *Software Architecture;*
- *Architectural Styles;*
- *Basic User Interface Design;*
- *Object Oriented Design;*
- *Structured System Design;*
- *Coding principles*

The practical applications of the topics are discussed for generating further curiosity and creativity as well as improving problem solving capacity.

Besides giving multiple choice questions as well as questions of short and long answer types marked in two categories following lower and higher order of Bloom's taxonomy, assignments, a list of references and suggested readings are given in the unit so that one can go through them for practice. It is important to note that for getting more information on various topics of interest some QR codes have been provided in different sections which can be scanned for relevant supportive knowledge.

After the related practical, based on the content, there is a "Know More" section. This section has been carefully designed so that the supplementary information provided in this part becomes beneficial for the users of the book. This section mainly highlights the initial activity, examples of some interesting facts, analogy, history of the development of the subject focusing the salient observations and finding, timelines starting from the development of the concerned topics up to the recent time, applications of the subject matter for our day-to-day real life or/and industrial applications on variety of aspects, case study related to environmental, sustainability, social and ethical issues whichever applicable, and finally inquisitiveness and curiosity topics of the unit.

RATIONALE

Software design is the process of finding solutions to the problem stated by the customer. The input to the software design is the software requirements specification(SRS). The software Requirement specification specifies the expected functionalities and features of the system, and the software design translates the customer's requirements into a suitable form that helps the programmer to develop a source that can be later tested and deployed.

The challenge for the designers is to transform the requirements into a suitable design that helps implement the system. This is possible by following a systematic process. The software design process consists of a set of principles and practices that helps the designers to model the solution so that the product is developed and deployed as per the stakeholder's expectations.

Software design is classified into two types, high-level and the detailed design. The artifact of the high-level design is the software architecture which models the system's structure. The parts of the system and their connectors have to be identified and connected. The system may be built on the available patterns called architectural styles. The software architecture is decided based on the desired quality characteristics of the system.

The system can be decomposed into modules in the detailed design, and the interfaces to access these modules are also designed. The user interfaces that stakeholders use to access system's services are designed. The detailed design also includes the algorithm and data structure design.

A structured-system design or object-oriented designe is used depending on the target environment in which the system will be deployed. Once the design is ready, it can be converted to the source code. The source code should follow certain principles, which include simplicity, readability, modifiability, interoperability etc.

This unit helps students to understand the software design process. This includes architectural design, user-interface design, and object-oriented design. This unit also presents the coding principles that help in developing quality products.

PRE-REQUISITES

Computer Programming (Diploma Semester-III)

Scripting Languages (Diploma Semester-III)

UNIT OUTCOMES

List of outcomes of this unit is as follows:

U3-O1: Understand the software design concepts

U3-O2: Understand the software architecture and architectural styles

U3-O3: Understand User Interface Design principles

U3-O4: Understand object-oriented and structured design paradigms.

U3-O5: Understand the Coding Principles

Unit-3 Outcomes	EXPECTED MAPPING WITH COURSE OUTCOMES (1- Weak Correlation; 2- Medium correlation; 3- Strong Correlation)				
	CO-1	CO-2	CO-3	CO-4	CO-5
U3-O1	2	1	3	2	2
U3-O2	2	1	3	3	2
U3-O3	2	1	2	3	2
U3-O4	2	1	3	2	2
U3-O5	2	1	2	3	2

3.1 DESIGN PRINCIPLES

Software design is a process of defining the structural components, the interfaces, and the detailed design of the system. During the design phase, the system's structure is identified, and the functional requirements stated by the customer are realized. Hence, the design is a critical process. If the errors go unnoticed, it becomes difficult to correct them. Therefore, a specific set of principles must be followed to design a system. The inability to follow the design principles results in a system that is complex and difficult to maintain. To evaluate the design, the following properties have to be satisfied.

- Verifiable : To check whether each requirement stated is designed
- Efficient : The system uses optimal resources in a better way. An efficient system consumes fewer resources.
- Simple : The design should be easy to understand.
- Maintainable: The design should be modifiable; that is, any future change requests should be incorporated
- Traceable : Each design construct should be tracked with the requirements stated.

3.1.1 Problem Decomposition and Hierarchy

Large problems are often difficult to solve as they are complex. The complexity can be reduced if it is divided into sub-problems using the divide and conquer strategy. The design goal is to divide the problem into manageable sub-problems that can be realized effectively. A complex system can be partitioned into several components that can be further decomposed into any level till the parts are easy to understand and model. The partitioning or decomposing can stop once the parts are simple enough to be realized. The designer has to generally make a judgment as to when to stop partitioning.

The decomposition of the problem into several subproblems results in problem partitioning that can be represented as a hierarchy of components. The simpler components be solved and aggregated to implement a sub-problem. For example, if the function "f" is complex, it can be divided into sub-functions (f_1 and f_2). The functions f_1 and f_2 can then be aggregated to realize the function "f". Each component at the lowest level of the hierarchy is easy to understand, test, and modify.

3.1.2 Abstraction

Abstraction is the most critical part of the design process and is essential for problem decomposition. It is a tool that that allows the designer to consider components at the abstract level where the underlying details are not be specified.

To start the design any system, it is imperative to define an abstract component, which may not specify the inner level details at the initial level to understand the problem well. A single level of abstraction is generally sufficient for simple problems. However, for complex problems, there can be various levels of abstraction.

Generally, there are two types of abstraction mechanisms used in software systems, the functional abstraction and the data abstraction. In the functional abstraction, the problem is partitioned into various functions. The decomposition of the problem is in terms of functional modules of system that specify the functionalities without specifying the implementation details. Functional abstraction is the basis for structured design.

In data abstraction, a system is visualized as a set of real-time objects, and each object provides specific services. In data abstraction, the internals of objects are hidden, and only the services of the object are visible. Data abstraction forms the basis of the object oriented design.

3.1.3 Modularity

The modular system consists of well-defined, manageable components or units that interact with each other through well-defined interfaces. The system should be partitioned into modules in such a way that each such division is discrete, which can be implemented and well maintained. The following set of principles can be followed to achieve better modularity.

- Each module is well-defined and can be used by any other application (reusability).
- A module should be separately compiled and stored in a library.
- Modules can call other modules.
- Modules should be simple so that it is easier to understand and maintain.

Effective modularity allows the system to divide it into various parts, each being developed by separate development teams. Further, it also helps to track the design and development progress. It also helps in testing the individual parts of the system.

However, If the modularisation is not done correctly, it may lead to several problems. This includes increased intermodular communication, and problems with integration.

3.2 MODULAR DESIGN

The modular design helps reduce the system's complexity and allows the development of various parts of the systems parallelly, as the modules are generally discrete. In modular design, the modules are arranged hierarchically.

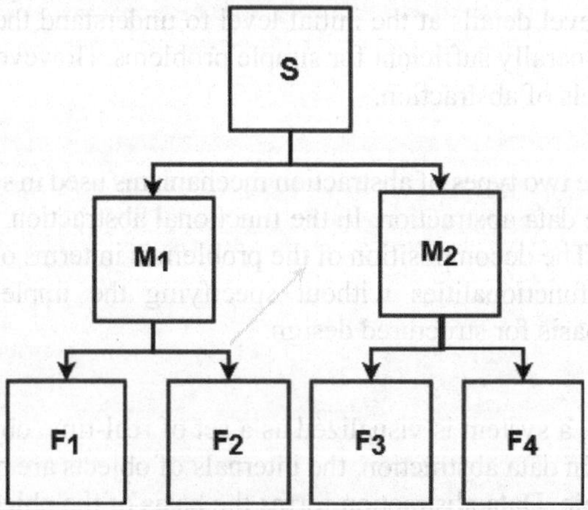

Fig. 3.1: Layered design

The first level of the hierarchy includes the names of the modules, and the lower level layers of the hierarchy represent the functions of the modules. Separate teams can implement these modules. In Figure 3.1, the system "S" is divided into two modules, namely "M_1" and "M_2" respectively. Each module is further partitioned into respective functions. If the functions are complex, they can be further decomposed. As the modules in the given figure are discrete, these modules can be implemented parallelly by separate teams. The layered design helps in understanding the system easily. Each module can be tested and deployed, and if any errors are found, they can be debugged with ease. The factors that impact the design of the system are coupling and cohesion. A well-designed system is expected to have loose coupling and tight cohesion. Such modular systems are simple, modifiable, verifiable, traceable, and reusable.

3.2.1 Coupling

Coupling refers to the strength of the relationship between the modules of the system. Two modules of a system are said to be tightly coupled, i.e. the relationship between the modules is high when the modules are strongly dependent on each other. In tightly coupled systems, the modules cannot be separated as one depends on the part of the functionality of the other. Two modules that do not depend on each other or interact by passing only the primitive data items are said to be loosely coupled.

Coupling is classified into various types based on the strength of the interaction between the modules of the system. Figure 3.2 describes five types of coupling arranged in the increasing order of the relationship between the modules (loose to tight).

Data	**Stamp**	**Control**	**Common**	**Content**
Loose →				**Tight**
(Most Desirable)				**(Least Desirable)**

Fig. 3.2: Coupling types

- **Data Coupling:** Two modules, A and B, are said to be data coupled if they communicate by passing data of elementary type. For example, a data coupling exist between two functions f_1 and f_2 if there is a call to function f_2 from function f_1 using primitive data types. The parameters used in calling f_2 can be of the following types: integer, real, character, boolean, enumeration, or a pointer.

- **Stamp Coupling:** Two modules, A and B, are said to be stamped coupled if they communicate using composite data structures such as objects, structures, and unions.

- **Control Coupling:** Control coupling is said to exist between two modules if the data in one module, directs the instruction execution in another. This usually happens when the flag that is set in one module is used for the execution of instructions in the other module. In other words, the decision taken in module A is used for the execution of instructions in module B.

- **Common Coupling**: Common coupling exists between two modules when they share the global data items. The changes to the global data item will affect all the modules using it. Determining which module is responsible for the changes made to the global data item will be challenging.

- **Content Coupling**: Content coupling is said to exist between two modules when one module modifies the internal working of another module. For example, in C++, a friend class can access the private members of a class.

3.2.2 Cohesion

Cohesion refers to the strength of the relationship between the module elements. The elements or functions of modules are said to be tightly cohesive when the relationship between the functions of module is high. In Figure 3.1, there should be more interaction between F_1 and F_2 to realize the functionality of Module M_1. The module's functions have to cooperate to achieve the objective of the module.

Cohesion is classified into various types, and cohesion's strength increases from coincidental cohesion to functional cohesion. Figure 3.3 describes seven types of cohesion

Coincidental	Logical	Temporal	Procedural	Communicational	Sequential	Functional
Loose (Least Desirable) →						Tight (Most Desirable)

Fig. 3.3: Cohesion types

- **Coincidental cohesion:** Coincidental cohesion exists when there is no or little relationship between the module's functions. The module's functions perform certain operations unrelated to the operations of the other function within the same module.

- **Logical cohesion:** If the elements of the modules perform similar operations, then the module is said to be logically cohesive. Similar operations across the functions of a module include data input, output, exceptional handling, etc.

- **Temporal cohesion:** A module is said to exhibit temporal cohesion if the functions of the module are executed at a particular time. For example, the booting of a computer initiates execution of several functions simultaneously.

- **Procedural cohesion:** When the set of functions of a module are executed in a specific order, then the module is said to possess procedural cohesion. The functions are executed in a sequence but may not be related, or they may operate on different data.

- **Communicational cohesion:** A module is said to exhibit communicational cohesion if all functions of a module update the same data structure. For example, the push, pop, and peep operations are performed on a stack or a queue data structure.

- **Sequential cohesion**: Sequential cohesion exists between the functions of a module when these functions are executed in an order such that the output of one function becomes the input to another. For example, checking availability, placing an order, and payment are the functionalities of an e-commerce application which has to be executed in the same sequence. The output of one becomes the input of the other.

- **Functional cohesion**: When different functions of a module interact and coordinate to execute a task, the module is said to be functionally cohesive.

3.3 SOFTWARE ARCHITECTURE

The software architecture of a system represents the organization of systems consisting of a set of components and the interconnection between them. The architecture design is concerned with understanding how the overall system is organized. Architectural design is the first step in the software design process.

The software architecture generally consists of the following elements:

- Set of components that include database, libraries, or computational units, which are responsbile for implementing the system's services.
- Set of interfaces that connects various components for communication and coordination across the system.

The input to the architecture design process is the requirements specification, and the output of the architectural design is a well-defined software architecture. The proper choice of software architecture is needed as it affects the system's performance, maintainability, and robustness. The architectural design depends on the type of system being developed, the requirements of the customer, and the architect's experience. The desired non-functional requirements of the system characterize the architecture of the system.

Generally, each component implements the functional requirements given by the customer. But the non-functional characteristics are realized by the system's architecture. The architecture of the system is decided based on the desired non-functional characteristics. As these characteristics vary from one system to another, there can be multiple structures for the same system.

Suppose a system that takes student's feedback on teaching-learning-evaluation has to be developed. The student gives responses to various questions asked in the feedback. The architecture of the feedback system consists of three components: client, server, and database, as depicted in Figure 3.4.

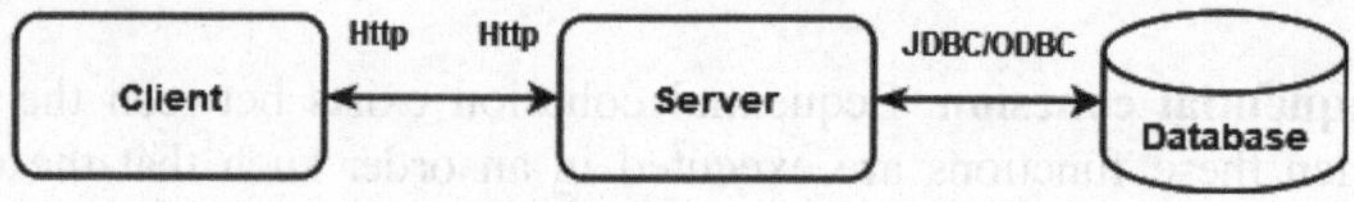

Fig. 3.4: Feedback system architecture

The client component is used to display the feedback form to the student. The student can give the responses to the questions and submit the same. The second component processes the data submitted by the student, does the required validation, and stores the result into the third component which is a database. These three components need to be connected. As the student submits the feedback, it is to be received by server for processing and the response has to be recorded in database. There is a need for communication channel between these components.

The components of this system are clients, server, and database. The clients can request for certain service to the server. The request is sent using HTTP to the server. The server, in turn, connects to the database using jdbc/odbc connectivity. After retrieving the required information from the database, the server returns the response to the client. The proposed student feedback architecture has yet to consider many of the quality characteristics of the system. For example, a student can give feedback any number of times for the same course and same semester, as there is no mechanism to authenticate the student. Another component namely authentication server, may be required in such a case. Similarly, the server or database may fail as the architecture did not consider the availability characterstics. We may require a backup server and a replicated database copy to achieve availability. Hence there is a need to consider the desired quality characteristics of the system, including performance, security, availability, reliability, maintainability, etc., and accordingly propose the software architecture.

If security is the desired non-functional or critical requirement, the layered structure may be used where the most critical elements are placed in the inner layer. Each layer may contain access to certain services and data. It is necessary that the producers of the data should be separated from the consumers of data, and shared data has to be avoided for easy maintenance.

If maintainability is the desired quality characteristic, the fine-grained components must be self-contained to adapt quickly. Further, the data producer should be separated from the consumers of data, and shared data has to be avoided for such components as maintenance becomes problematic.

If performance is the desired non-functional requirement, then the operations that affect the system's performance must be included in small components, which must be localized and should not be distributed. The architects use microservices to achieve the desired performance of the system.

3.4 ARCHITECTURAL STYLES

An architectural style describes principles, characteristics, and features that provide an abstract framework for a specific set of systems. This promotes design reuse by providing solutions to common problems called patterns. The basic idea behind architectural patterns is to describe and reuse the structures of software systems that have been adopted in similar domains.

For example, developing a portal for online shopping or online admission system, railway reservation system, etc., requires one to develop a web-based system. An architecture for a web-based system can be reused for all such systems.

Some of the most commonly used architectural styles are model-view-controller, layered, repository, client-server, and pipe and filter architectures.

3.4.1 Model-View-Controller (MVC) Architecture

The Model-View-Controller (MVC) architecture is divided into three components: model, view, and controller, which interact. This architecture is used when there is a need to separate the user interfaces from the system and data. The model component manages the data and the operations on it. The view component defines user interfaces that the user uses to give inputs to the system. The control component interfaces between the view, and the model components. It generally implements the business logic to realize the local validations based on the events at the view level, which includes button press, mouse click, mouse move, etc. The MVC architecture is depicted in Figure 3.5.

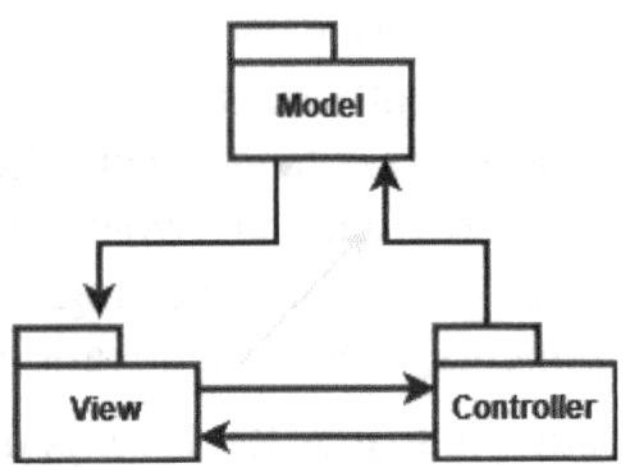

Fig. 3.5: Model-View-Controller architecture

The Model-View-Controller (MVC) architecture provides an abstract view of the system. The view components define how the data is displayed to the user. The controller updates the model or the view based on the input given by the user. The model defines the data required for a particular application, and whenever the state of the data changes it may notify it to the view.

Considering the feedback system example, the feedback form is displayed on the view component. The student fills out the feedback form and submits the same. The controller verifies whether any fields are missing. If so, it notifies the student. If the validation is successful, the information is updated in the database in the model component. The acknowledgment is given back to the student at the view level once the feedback is recorded.

3.4.2 Layered Architecture

The layered architecture supports the incremental development of the system. Components in the layered architecture are organized into a few horizontal layers such that each layer performs a specific task. There can be any number of layers based on the given requirement. However, the most commonly used layered architecture uses four standard layers. Fig 3.6 represent a generic layered architecture with four layers.

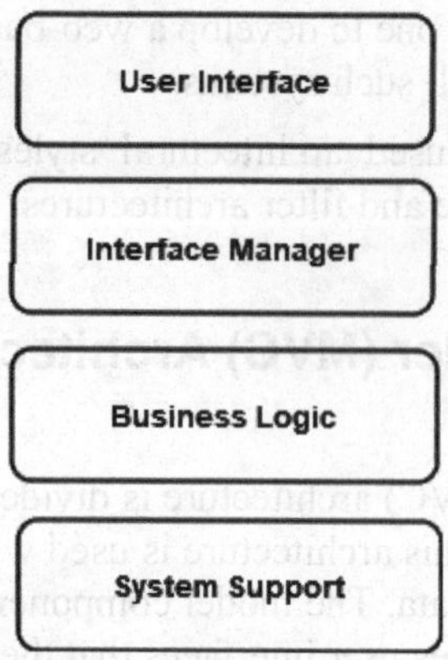

Fig. 3.6: Generic layered architecture

The lowest layer includes system support services that typically contains Operating system, databases, etc. This layer is also known as the database layer. The second layer is the business logic layer which contains components with system functionalities. The interface manager is responsible for authentication and authorization mechanisms. The topmost layer is the user interface layer which could be a browser from where the user interacts. The number of layers is arbitrary. Each layer can be further divided into two layers. Some of the layers can also be merged. For example, the interface manager and business logic layer can be merged into a middleware that provides functional components, user authentication, and authorization.

The advantage of this architecture is that as the layer is developed, some of the services provided by the layer may be available for users. The layer provides services to the layer above it. The lowest level represents the core services of the system.

This architecture is used when the development of the system is spread across teams, and each team is responsible for developing the functionality of a layer. Layered architecture is specifically used when there is a requirement for multi-level security where the innermost layer will have the most critical components.

The advantage of this architecture is that it allows the replacement of a layer as long as the user interface is not changed. However, the clear separation of concerns between different layers is challenging.

3.4.3 Repository Architecture

The repository architecture is also said to be a data-centered, or shared data style architecture. There are two components in the repository architecture. One is the central repository, and the other one is the data accessor. Fig 3.7 presents the repository architecture.

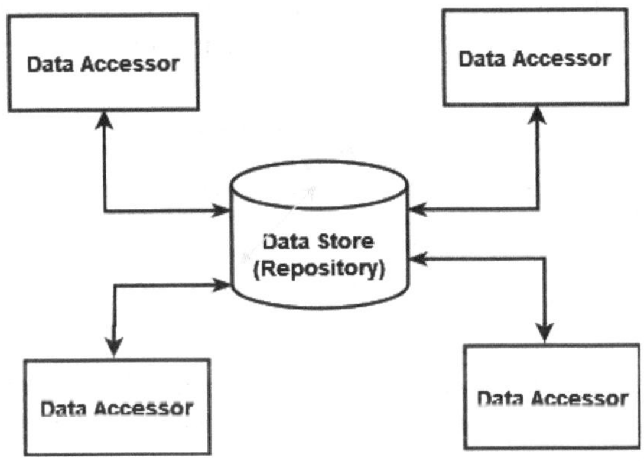

Fig. 3.7: Repository architecture

A data repository is a place where the system stores the shared data. This could be in the form of files, or databases. The data accessors are client applications that read the data from the repository, and process them. If the results of this data have to be shared, then these accessors will put the data back in the repository. Data accessors do not interact directly with each other. However, the interaction is only through shared data type through a data repository.

There are two variants of this architecture. In the first case, the repository is active, where once the shared data is modified, the accessor components are informed about it. The data accessor components are informed about the changes to the shared data. In the second variant, the repository is a passive repository, which only provides the storage of this data in the components, and the accessors have to access the data as per the requirements.

This architecture is used in current-day systems, where large volumes of information are stored for a long time. The data accessors can access the shared data based on their need for making decisions, getting insights into the data, etc., depending on their requirements. Each accessor could be a separate system that takes this data and makes appropriate decisions for their business.

The disadvantage of this architecture is that, as the shared data is stored in a single repository, any failures in this repository may put the system in a dormant state.

3.4.4 Client-Server Architecture

One of the commonly used architectures is the client-server style architecture, one of the basic distributed computing paradigms. There are two components of this architecture: client and server. The client component requests services remotely from any location and device. The server component processes the request of the clients by providing the services to the clients. The advantage of this architecture is that multiple clients from various locations can access the services at any time. The generic client-server architecture is presented in Figure 3.8.

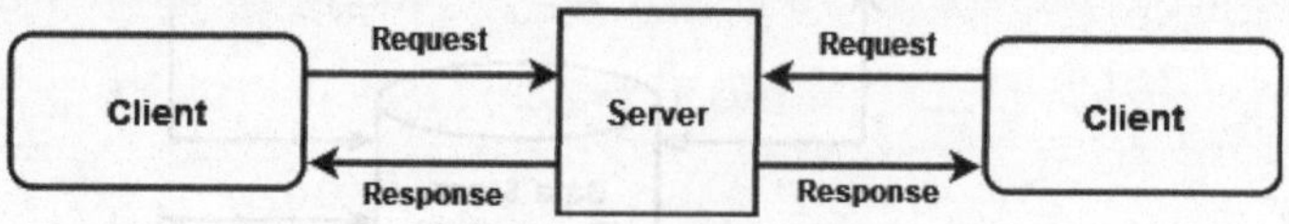

Fig. 3.8: Client-Server architecture

The client is a computer program that is used to request the desired service. Servers are software components that can run several services that respond to the client's request. The connection between the components is possible through a request-reply connector, which requires network connectivity.

Servers are software components that can run several services. Some of these services are realized by a set of servers where each is responsible for realizing a part of the service. One could be an application server, and another could be a database server. The general form of this architecture is n-tier architecture.

In a three-tier architecture (Fig 3.9), the client requests a service received by the second layer. The second layer is said to be a middle layer that contains business logic. In order to realize the request, the business layer may have to request the data from the database server. The third layer is the database server that maintains the database. The business layer interacts with the database server for all data-related queries.

Fig. 3.9: Three-tier architecture

3.4.5 Pipe and Filter Architecture

The pipe and filter architecture pattern is used when there is a function transformation between the various components of the system. There will be a flow from one competent to another component after its transformation in a sequence. These transformations may execute in sequential or parallel, and each component can process the data. The generic pipe and filter architecture is depicted in Figure 3.10

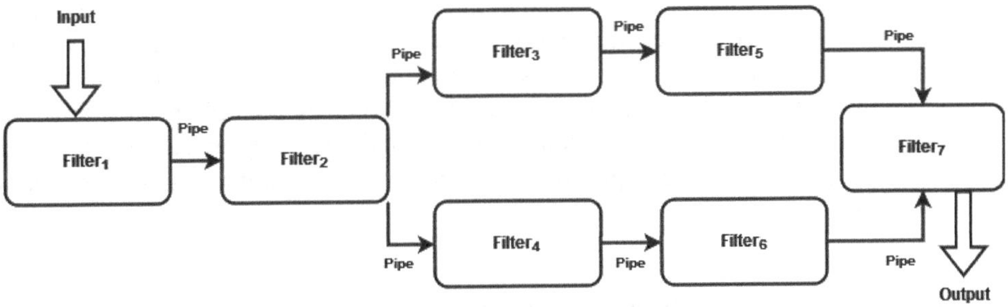

Fig. 3.10: Pipe and Filter architecture

The pipe and filter architecture has an independent component called a filter that performs data transmission by taking the input and producing an output that acts as an input to the next filter. Pipes serve as connectors between the filters. Data flows in a pipe from one filter to the other. This architecture connects components that process a data stream wherein one component is connected to another. In Figure 3.10, $filter_1$ and $filter_2$ are connected sequentially, whereas $filter_3$ and $filter_4$ are in parallel. The pipe is a unit action channel that cannot change the data in any manner but merely transmit from one filter to another filter. This architecture is used in data processing applications. This could be transactional-based or batch based, where a given input is processed in stages.

3.5 USER INTERFACE DESIGN

The user interface is the means of interaction with the system. The end users interact with the system through user interfaces. There is a need to develop these user interfaces systematically to realize the system's usability quality characteristics. The quality of the user's experience in interacting with the system is usability.

An interface that could be easier to use leads to satisfaction among customers. The system might implement all the desired functionalities of the customer. However, as a user interface is badly designed, the user may be unable to use the system functionality effectively. Because of its importance, the effort required to develop the user interface is high.

Generally, there are two user interfaces, a Command Line Interface (CLI) and a Graphical User Interface (GUI). In the command line interface, a command prompt is provided where the user enters the commands given to the system. The user needs to remember the usage of commands in order to give the request. The command line interface is easier to develop than the graphical user interface. The command language interface can be systematically developed using standard tools like Lex and YACC. Command line interfaces are generally difficult to learn as the user has to memorize the command, and users may make errors in typing those commands.

On the other hand, Graphical user interfaces are easy to use. The Graphical Interface provides a simple visual representation that is used to interact with the system. It is also known as a menu-based interface. In these interfaces, the typing effort is minimal, and the user interacts with the system through icons and by selecting several options. The graphical user interface is designed based on the customer's knowledge and background. The user should be able to navigate various menus and select the appropriate options. Though GUI interfaces are easy to use, the experts may find it difficult as they can type commands faster on a command line interface and get the computation done quickly.

3.5.1 User Interface Design Process

The first step is identifying the users' interaction skills with the system. Accordingly, the users may be classified into various categories based on their technical knowledge. The UI design may differ from one type of user to another as the design may be specific to the type of user. Then the tasks that each user category can perform must be specified and elaborated. The devices on which these users will be accessing the interfaces and the environmental effects on interfaces have to be considered.

In the second step, the objects of the interface design are identified. The tasks are listed sot hat the elements of the user interface design to implement the tasks are identified. Error handling and help facilities for each task must be listed. This step has to be iterated until all the desired features or tasks are captured.

The third step is the interface implementation phase. In this step, the prototype model specifying all the scenarios stated based on the user requirements is presented user interface. It consists of the creation of windows, menus, forms, scroll bars, messages, commands, etc. This step is iterated till the user accepts the prototype.

In the fourth step, once the operational user interface is ready, the user interface is tested to check whether all the requirements stated in the software requirements specification are included. In an object-oriented paradigm, a user interface generally exists between the actor and a use case. Similarly, in the structured paradigm, user interfaces are created between the external entity and the process of the system.

3.5.2 User Interface Design Principles

The following principles are to be followed for a better user interface design:

- The user interface would be simple so that the user can navigate the interfaces easily.
- The user must be provided with mechanisms to navigate using a keyboard, mouse, or touch screen effectively. There is a need to provide all types of interactions.
- The user interface is expected to be attractive with proper colors, buttons, etc, such that it should be easy to use and visualize.
- There should be consistency in user interface design across various system interfaces.
- There should not be aware of the internal technical details of the system. The user only interacts with interfaces by giving inputs to the system.
- Shortcuts to use various objects of the user interface have to be provided wherever possible.
- There is a need to provide a proper help facility so that the user can access the UI seamlessly. This may include quick access to help files, tooltip provision, etc.

3.6 OBJECT ORIENTED DESIGN

Object-oriented software development is a popular paradigm widely used because of its features. It helps develop modularized components that can be easily maintained and reused. An effective object-oriented design for a given problem is possible by building several models that are iterated to make a design that can be easily translated to the source code. The object-oriented design follows a bottom-up approach to realizing the solution to the given problem.

Unified Modeling Language (UML) is a de facto standard for writing software blueprints for object-oriented systems. The model helps in visualizing the system in a better way and in realizing the system as per expectations. UML is a language for visualizing, specifying, constructing, and documenting. The basic building blocks of UML are things, relationships, and diagrams.

The deliverables of the object-oriented analysis phase are use case models with specifications and analysis classes. In object-oriented design, each use case is realized. A use case realization indicates how a use case will be implemented. The realization requires the identification of objects and their interactions.

3.6.1 Interaction Diagram

An interaction specifies the system's dynamic behavior in which different elements collaborate and interact. The primary element of an object-oriented paradigm is an object. An *object* is a real-time entity with a state, behavior, and identity.

The state of an object represents its characteristics or properties. The behavior represents the operations that can be performed on the given object. Each object is distinguishable and has an identity. An object can have a name (Named object) or be represented as an instance of a class (anonymous object). The representation of an object is given in Fig 3.11

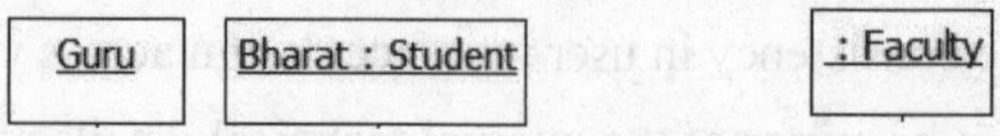

(a) Named Object (b) Anonymous Object

Fig. 3.11: Object representation

An interaction diagram is used to model the exchange of messages between the objects of a system. There are two types of interaction diagrams: Sequence diagrams and Collaboration diagrams.

A *Sequence diagram* is an interaction diagram that depicts the time ordering of messages. The messages are temporally modeled. In a sequence diagram, the objects are arranged on X-axis, and Y-axis represents the time dimension. The general format of the sequence diagram is given in Fig. 3.12

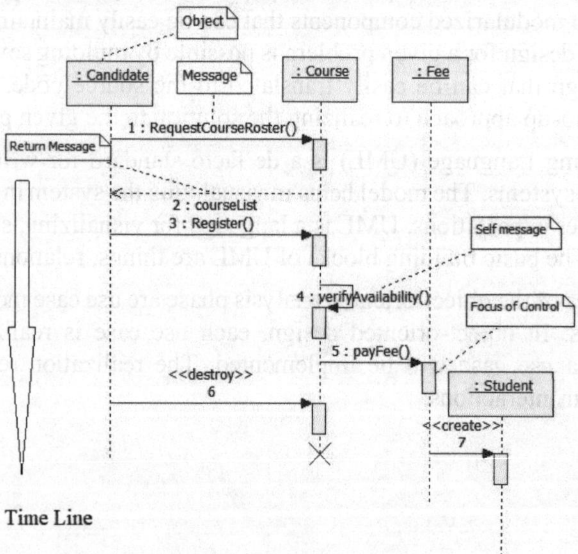

Fig. 3.12: Sequence diagram

One object communicates with the other by passing messages. Communication can be passing messages between objects, self-messages, returning messages, and creating and destroying the objects. In Fig 3.12, the objects Candidate, Course, and Fee are represented along the X-axis. The objects communicate by passing messages. There can be a self message which is generally used for local validation. Each object has a lifeline (dotted line). After the expiry of the lifeline, the object is automatically destroyed. The objects can also be destroyed explicitly before the expiry of the lifeline. This is possible by sending a destroy message (X). The *focus of control* represents the time required to execute the message. The Candidate, Course, and Fee objects are created at the same time. However, the Object Student is dynamically created by executing a create message.

Each scenario of the use case can be modeled using the sequence diagrams. Firstly, various objects required to realize the use cases are identified, and the sequence diagram is modeled. The messages are later transformed into the methods of the respective classes.

A collaboration diagram (also known as a communication diagram) is an interaction diagram that depicts structural organization. Unlike sequence diagrams, the collaboration diagram has a direct link between the objects. Sequence diagrams and collaboration diagrams are semantically equivalent. A given sequence diagram can be converted to a collaboration diagram. The equivalent collaboration diagram of the sequence diagram(Fig.3.12) is given in Fig 3.13.

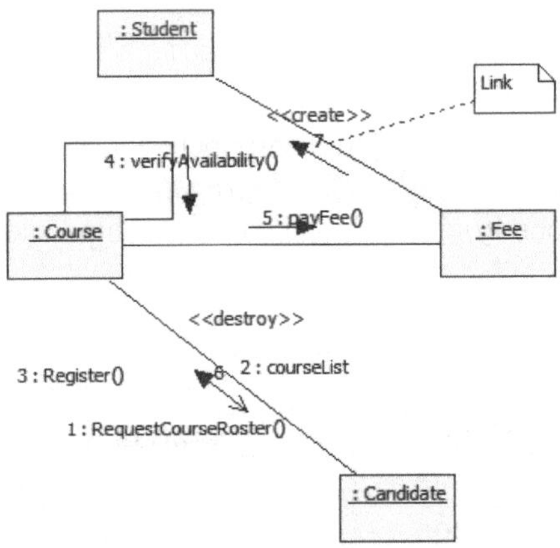

Fig. 3.13: Collaboration diagram

In the collaboration diagram, there is a direct link between the objects. However, the object's life line and focus of control is not explicitly stated. The organization of the collaboration diagram is a structural organization.

3.6.2 Class Diagram

During the analysis phase, the classes were identified using a Noun convention or a CRC card method. These classes are designed by identifying the properties and respective methods. Each message passed between the objects becomes the method of the class.

A class diagram represents a static view of the system. It represents a set of classes, interfaces, and relationships between them. Class diagrams are used not only for visualizing and specifying but also for developing systems. The resultant class diagram can be converted into the source code. A generic class diagram is shown in Figure 3.14.

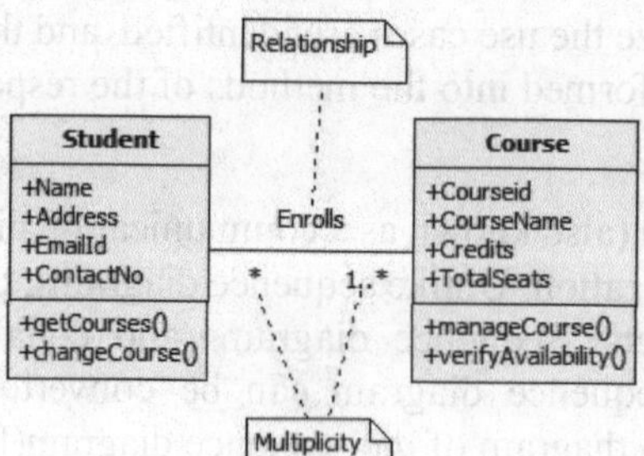

Fig. 3.14: Generic Class diagram

A class diagram specifies the relationship between the classes. Class relationships can be association, generalization, realization, aggregation, and composition. The relationship also specifies name, multiplicity, and role. The relationships used in the object-oriented design are given in Fig. 3.15

Relationship	Notation
Dependency	- - - - - - - - - - - - ->
Association	———————
Generalization	———————▷
Realization	- - - - - - - - - - - ▷
Aggregation	———————◇
Composition	———————◆

Fig. 3.15: Relationships and their notations

A dependency relationship exists between two classes when the changes to one class affects the other. The association is the structural relationship between two classes. It shows the number of instances of a class related to the other. The association can be uni-directional or bidirectional.

Generalization is used to describe the relationship between base and derived classes. The derived class inherits the properties and behavior of the base class. It is also known as IS-A relationship (OR- relationship).

Realization is a relationship where one thing specifies a contract, and the other realizes it. The relationship between an interface and a class or component is realization, as a class or a component implements the interface.

Aggregation is a type of association relationship which is a whole-part or "And" relationship. The parts can exist independently, but together may represent another class. For example, Computer is a Class that can be aggregated using Keyboard, Mouse, and CPU classes which form parts of the Computer. The parts can exist independently. Composition is a type of association that is a whole-part relationship, but the whole and part of the class cannot be separated. If a person represents the whole in a composition relationship, its parts could be the Head, leg, and body. If the person does not exist, the parts also do not remain.

The multiplicity represents the number of instances of one class relative to the other. There can be different variants of multiplicity. It can be one-to-one, one-to-many, and many-to-many with optional and mandatory relationships. Additionally, it can be represented in any valid range of values. For example, 2..10 represents a minimum of two instances and a maximum of 10 instances of the class. The variants of multiplicities are represented in Fig 3.16.

Multiplicty	**Description**
1..1	Only one (mandatory)
0..*	Zero or more (optional)
1..*	One or more (mandatory)
0..1	Zero or one (optional)
m..n	Atleast m instances at atmost n instances

Fig. 3.16: Multiplicity variants

3.6.3 Case Study: Object Oriented Design

In section 2.3.2, an Indian Bank System is analyzed. The three primary use cases identified are Deposit Amount, Withdraw Amount, and Transfer Amount. The specifications of these use cases are given, and analysis classes are identified.

In object-oriented design, each of these use cases is realized. In all three use cases, the actor is the Teller. There is a need for user interface design between each actor to a use case. The user interfaces are realized as boundary class objects. The classes identified during the analysis phase can be at the backend. These are realized as entity class objects. The control class objects realize the interaction between boundary and entity class objects. The interaction diagrams model the scenarios of the use cases. There can be separate sequence diagrams for each scenario.

A user interface must be designed for the deposit amount and withdraw amount use case. The generic user interface for Deposit amount is given in Fig. 3.17.

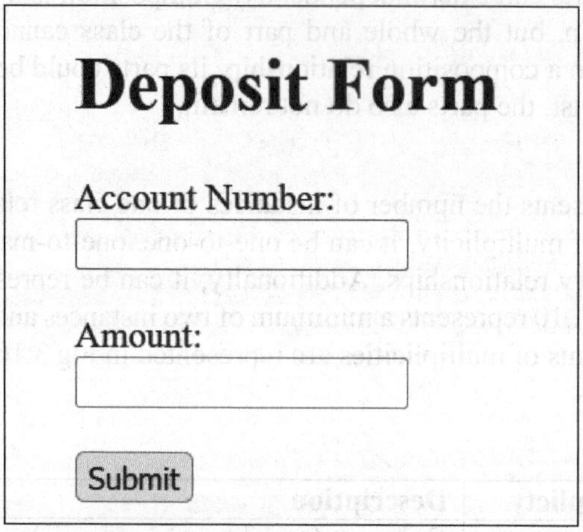

Fig. 3.17: Deposit Amount User Interface

It is clear from the user case specification of Deposit Amount that the required fields in the UI for Deposit form are Account number and Amount. The local validations must be performed on the Account number (number of digits) and valid Amount.

In the sequence diagrams for the scenarios of a use case, the first object is that of the user interface, which is also said to be a boundary class object. Once the form is filled, it is submitted to the controller object. This acts as an interface between the boundary and the entity class objects.

The sequence diagram for the deposit amount is specified in Fig.3.18. The Teller fills out the Deposit form and submits it. The local validation can be specified on each text box to check the valid account number and Amount, or the validations can be specified on the submit button.

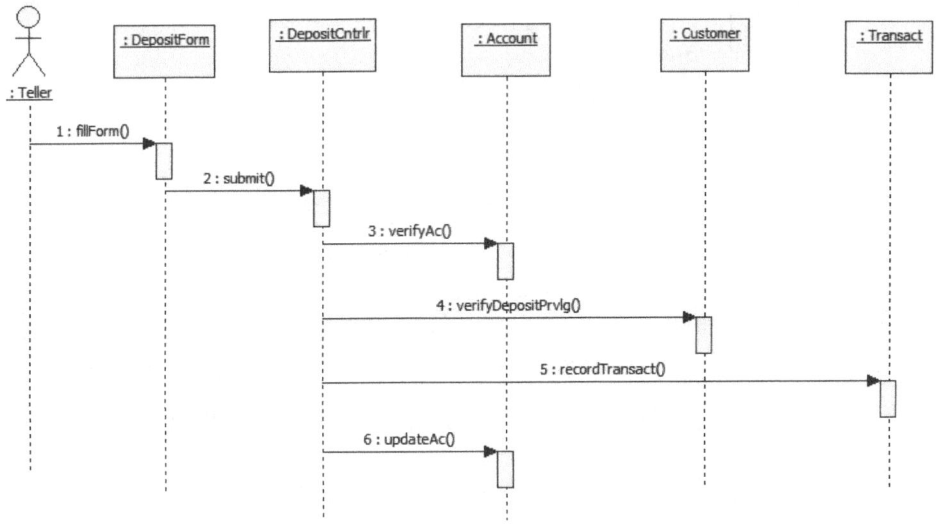

Fig. 3.18: Sequence diagram for Deposit Amount

The Account, Customer, and Transact objects are at the back end (or database). They are entity class objects in which the information is stored longer. The methods which are exchanged between the objects correspond to the sequence of activities specified in the use case specification of the deposit amount.

Similarly, there will be user interfaces for withdrawal amount and transfer amount. The sequence diagram for the withdraw amount is specified in Fig. 3.19.

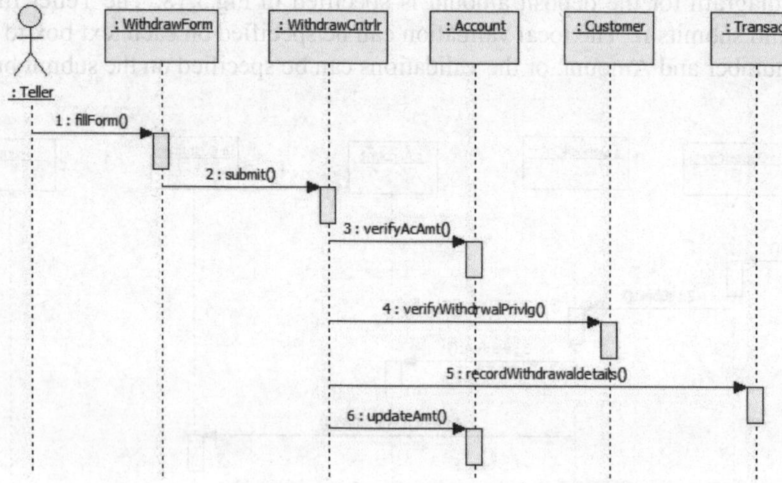

Fig. 3.19: Sequence diagram for Withdraw Amount

The sequence diagram for transfer amount is specified in Fig. 3.20.

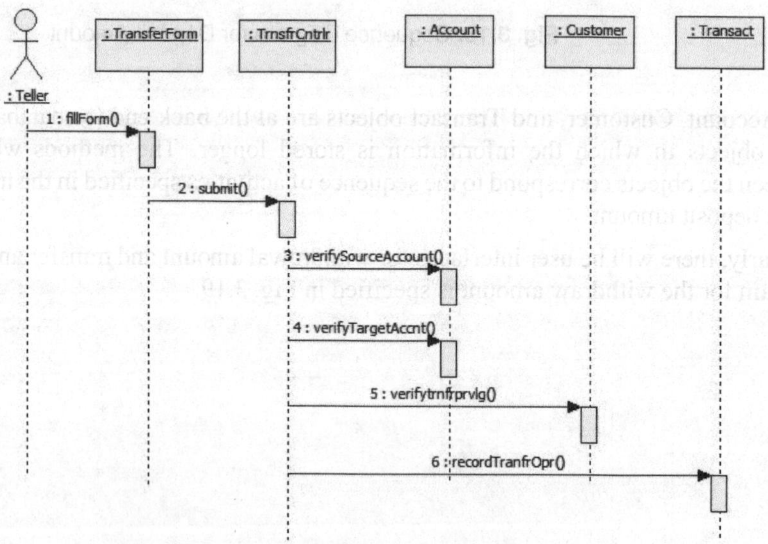

Fig. 3.20: Sequence diagram for Tranfer Amount

Each message that is modeled in the sequence diagram becomes the method of the target class. For example, in Fig. 3.20, 'verifySourceAccount()' is the message sent from the TranfrCntrlr object to the object of Account Class, then 'verifySourceAccount()' becomes the method of the Account Class. As sequence diagrams and collaboration diagrams are semantically equivalent, one can generate the equivalent collaboration diagrams for the above-specified scenarios.

The data structures and algorithms need to be designed in a detailed design. For each of the class's attributes, its type, initial value, range of values, etc., need to be modeled. Similarly, the return type, parameter list, parameter types, etc, have to be modeled for the class methods. Further, all the user interfaces can be packaged as a client. The controller objects can be packaged into a middleware with business logic, and the entity objects can be packaged into a server, thus facilitating a three-tier architecture. The class diagram involving the entity classes in the above scenario is given in Fig 3.21.

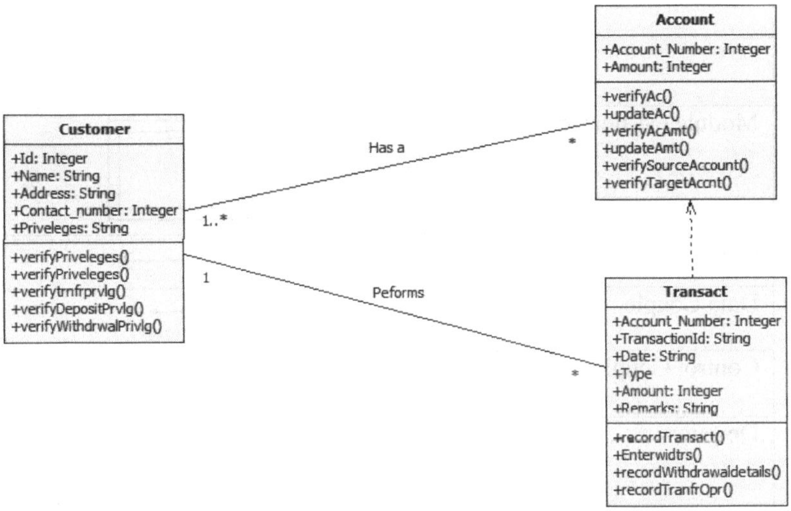

Fig. 3.21: Class diagram for the Banking System

3.7 STRUCTURED SYSTEM DESIGN

Structured System Design (SSD) aims to conceptualize a problem into interacting modules. Each module has a clear set of sub-modules or functions that interact to realize its objective. A system is said to be structured if it possesses loose coupling and tight cohesion. The structured system or function-oriented design aims to realize the solutions suitable for procedural languages.

The structured system design aims to transform the artifacts of structured analysis, a Data Flow Diagram (DFD), into a structure chart. Transform Analysis and Transaction Analysis are the two methods used to transform a DFD into a structure chart.

3.7.1 Structue Chart

The artifact of the structured or function-oriented design is a structure chart. A structure is a graphical representation of modules of a system and its relationship. Each module may contain several functions. The notations used to draw a structure chart are represented in Fig 3.22.

Name	Notation
Module (User-defined)	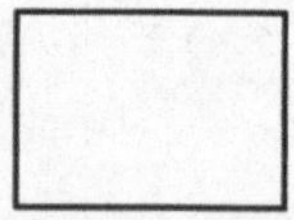
Module (System-defined)	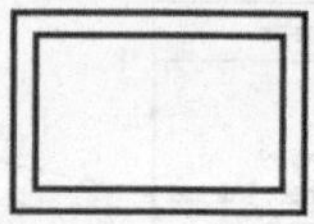
Call	
Data Couple	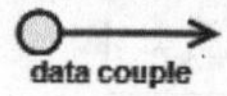
Control Couple	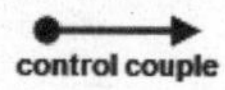
Decision	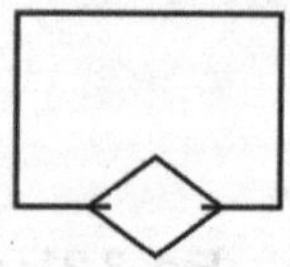
Iteration	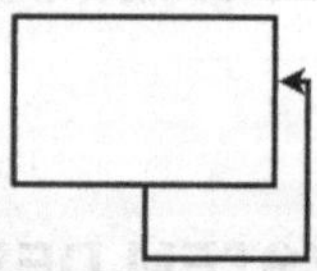

Fig. 3.22: Notations used in structure chart

A user-defined module is represented in a rectangle with the module's name inside it. The system-defined modules are represented in a double rectangle. A module can invoke or call another module. An arrow represents this. When a module calls another module, it may either pass data or control information between them. This is represented by data and control couple, respectively.

The decision taken in a given module may invoke other sub-modules, a decision box at the bottom of the rectangle represents this. The entire module may have to be iterated several times. A self-arrow to the module represents this.

3.7.2 Transform Analysis

One of the methods to convert a data flow diagram into a structure chart is transform analysis. The input, output, and transformation processes are identified and converted to a structure chart in tranform analysis. The procedure for transform analysis is as follows:

- Refine the data flow diagram

  The data flow diagram drawn during requirements analysis differs from the one drawn in the structured design. A data flow diagram is modeled in requirements analysis to understand the problem domain. During structured design, the data flow diagram shows the primary functions of the software. Transform analysis is used in simple applications where given input(s) are processed, and consequently, the output is generated.
  The refined data flow diagram of section 2.3.4 is represented in Fig. 3.23.

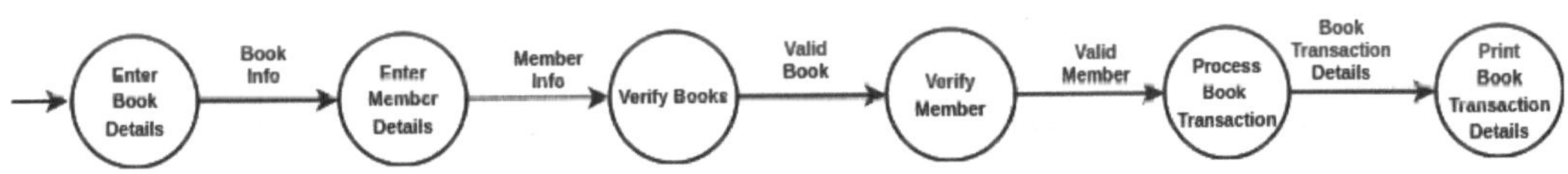

Fig. 3.23: DFD of LIS

- Identify the input and output boundaries in the data flow diagram.

  In this step, the goal is to separate the inputs, transforms, and outputs. The input area of the DFD includes all the processes that transform the input into the logical form. The input area is called an afferent branch. Similarly, the output area of DFD may convert the output area to physical form. The output area is also known as the efferent branch. The other processes in DFD perform the core transformations (also known as central transforms). The DFD with input and output boundaries is represented in Fig. 3.24.

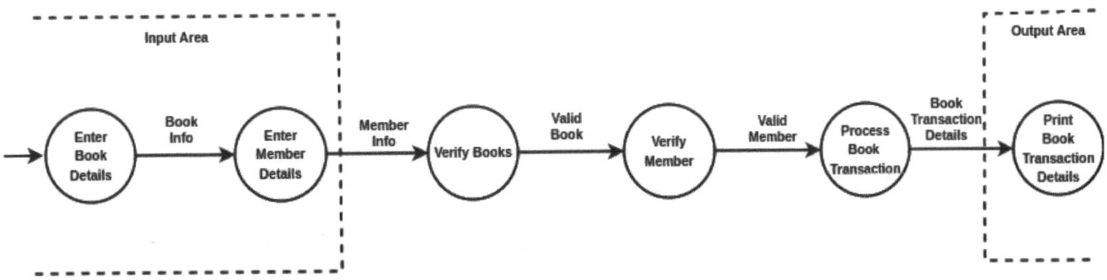

Fig. 3.24: DFD of LIS specifying the afferent and efferent branches

- First-level factoring
  Once the input and output boundaries are identified, the structure chart has sub-ordinate modules representing functional components of afferent, efferent, and transform processes represented in Fig 3.25.

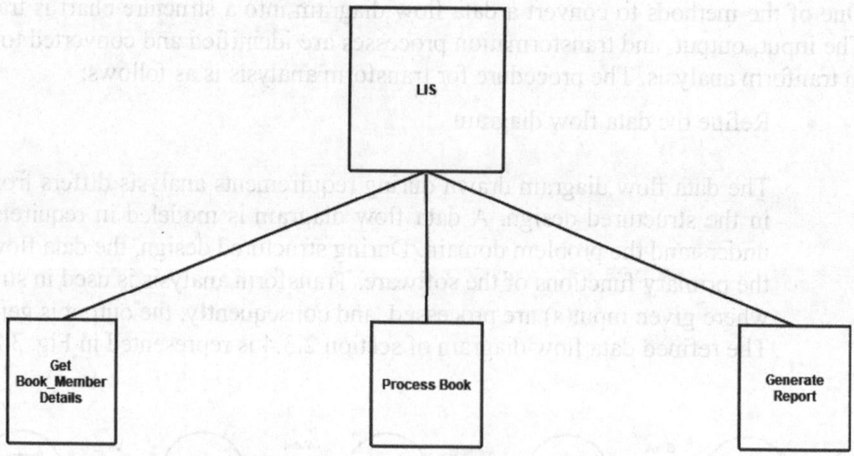

Fig. 3.25: Structure chart of LIS with first-level factoring

- Factoring of afferent, efferent and tranform branches.
  In this step, the structure chart is refined by adding sub-functions to the first-level modules. All the processes in the afferent area become the sub-functions of the afferent module. Similarly, the processes in the efferent area become sub-functions of the efferent module, and the remaining processes become the sub-functions of the transform module. Furthermore, the data and control information flowing between the modules is modeled. The resultant structure chart is given in Fig 3.26.

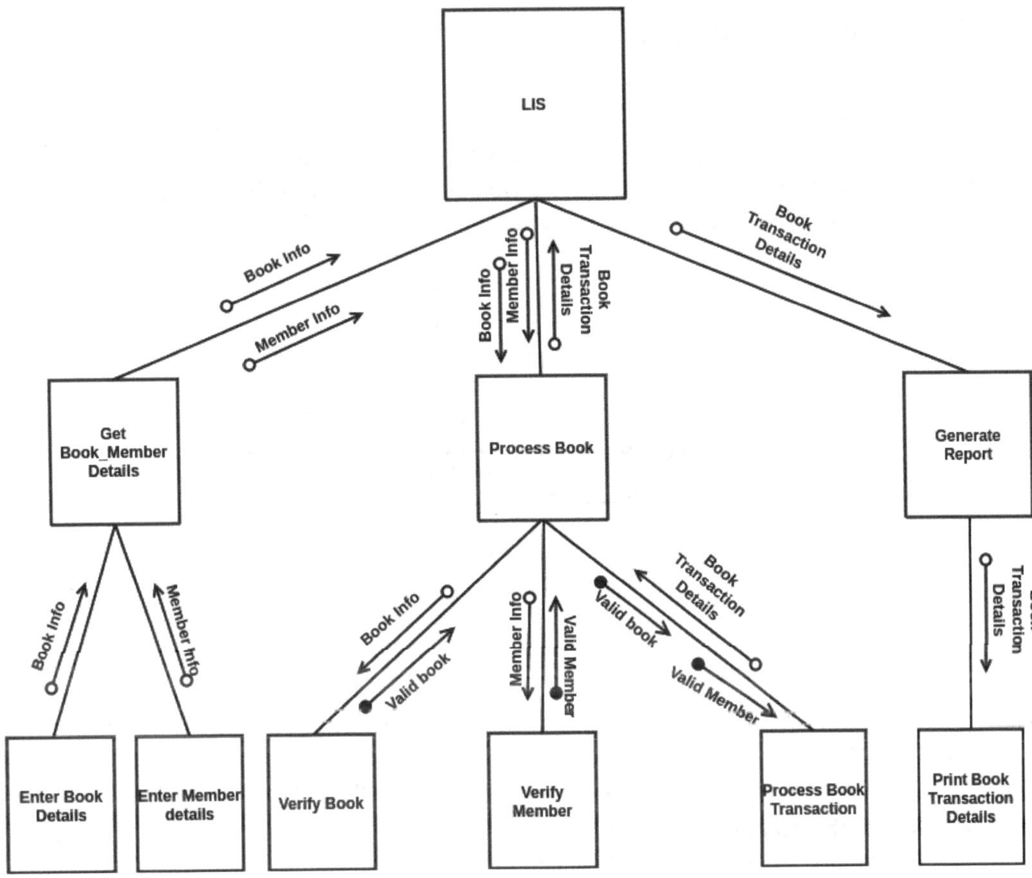

Fig. 3.26: Structure chart of LIS

The structure chart can be easily transformed into the target procedural language. Enter_ Book_details and Enter_Member_details are the functions used for taking inputs from the users and storing the same in files. Get_Member_Details will be a user-defined header file containing functions Enter_Book_Details and Enter_Member_Details.

Similarly, Verify_Book, Verify_Member, and Process_Book_Transactions are the functions implementing the core functionalities of LIS and Process_Book is a user-defined header file containing these functions. Print_Book_Transaction_Details is the function used to generate output, and other functions for the generting reports can be a part of the Generate_Report user-defined header file.

3.7.3 Transaction Analysis

Transaction analysis is a method to convert a data flow diagram to a structure chart. It is used when the tasks are invoked based on the inputs; generally, these tasks are independent. In transaction analysis, each input is used for different computation paths. The general form of the data flow diagram for transaction analysis is given in Figure 3.27.

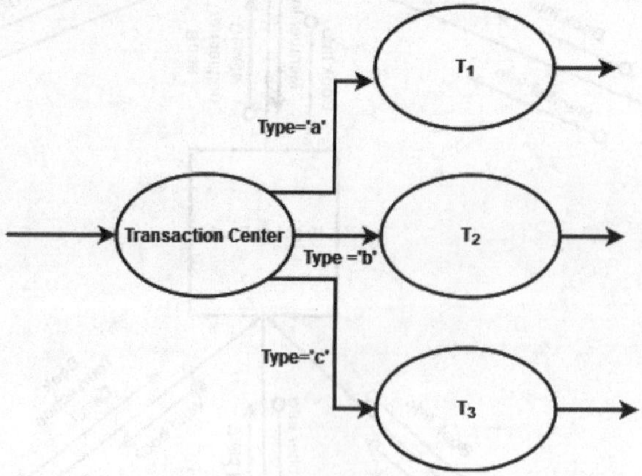

Fig. 3.27: DFD representing transaction analysis

The transaction centre takes input from the user, and based on the user's choice, the respective computation path contains sub-processes used to realize a given functionality. The following steps are followed to convert a DFD of transaction analysis into a structure chart.

- Refine the data flow diagram

  In the first step, the data flow diagram is refined to have a transaction centre and corresponding computational paths. The data flow diagram for the Indian Bank scenario (section 2.3.2) is given in Fig. 3.28.

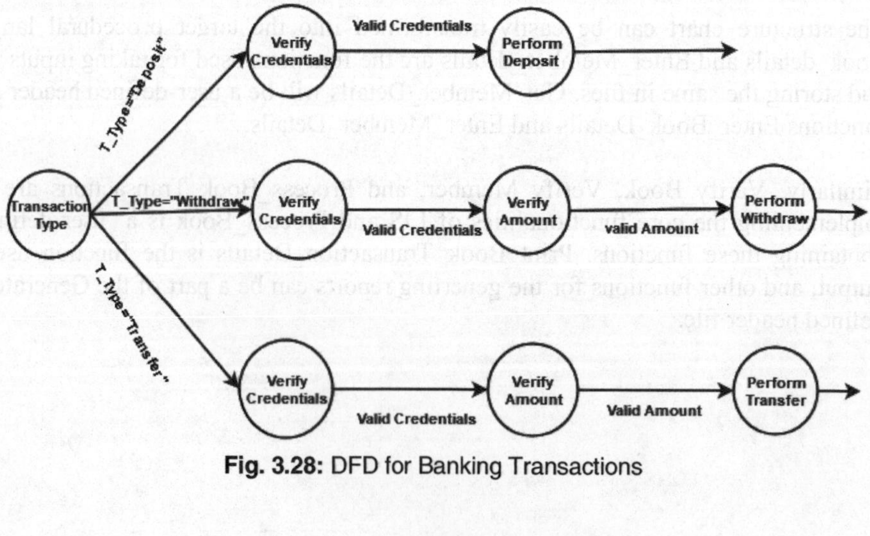

Fig. 3.28: DFD for Banking Transactions

- First level factoring
  The structure chart contains two subordinate modules in first-level factoring: the input and the dispatcher. The dispatcher module is used to realize different transaction paths. The execution of transaction paths terminates by updating all the master files at the end.
- Factoring of input and transaction sub-processes.
  In this step, the structure chart is refined by adding sub-functions to the input and dispatcher modules. The input module collects the user's input to identify a particular transaction flow. The dispatcher modules pass on other required inputs to perform computation, and finally, the master_files are updated. The data and control information flowing between the modules is modeled. The resultant structure chart is given in Fig 3.29.

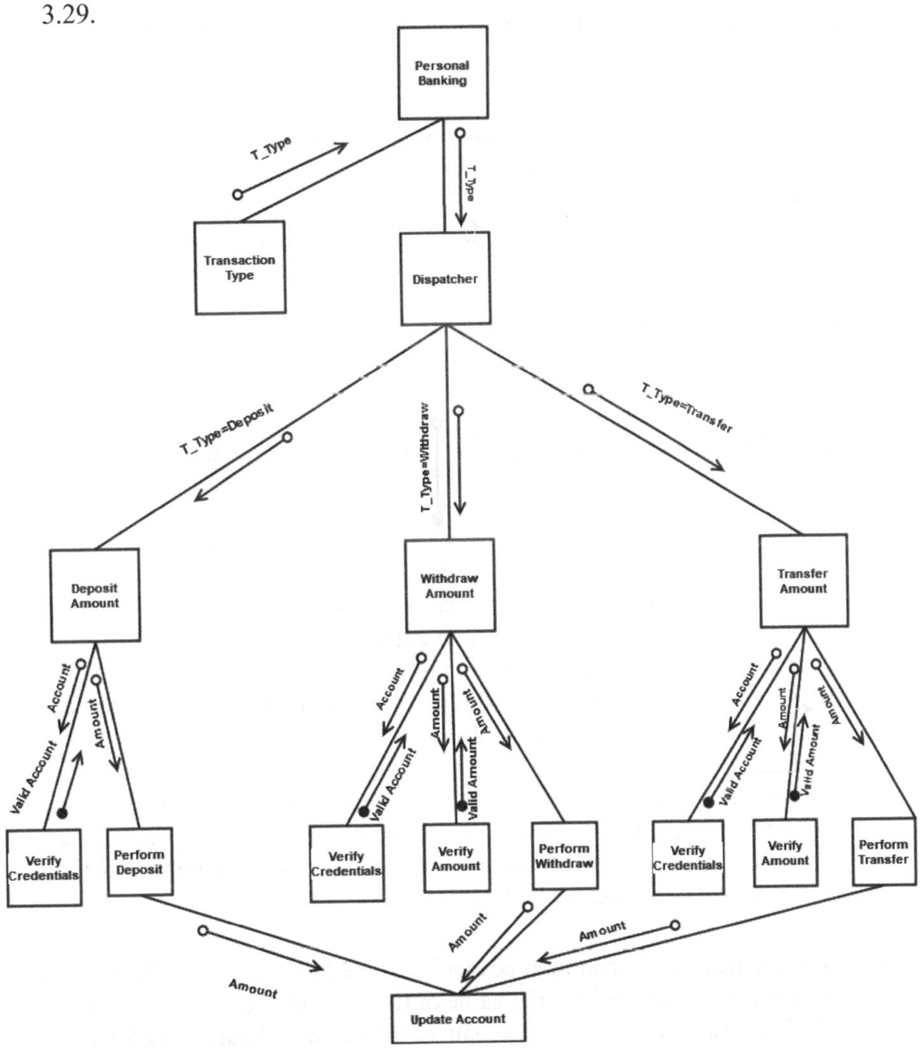

Fig. 3.29: Structure chart for Banking Transactions

3.8 CODING PRINCIPLES

The goal of the coding phase is to transform the design into the source code of the target programming language. The modules and functions identified during the design are converted to the source code by implementing appropriate data structures and algorithms. The functions of a module are first implemented, and later, the modules are integrated to realize the system's functionality. The agile software development approach uses pair programming, where two programmers work together to code and test the user stories.

The goal of coding is not only to transform the design into the source code but to develop quality programs. The quality of source code is expected to possess the following characteristics:

- Readability: The code is easy to read
- Reusability: The parts of the code should be easy to reuse
- Maintainability: The code should be able to make modifications and add new features
- Robustness: The code that can handle unexpected inputs
- Reliable: The code that does not produce dangerous failures.

3.8.1 Coding standards and guidelines

Coding standards and guidelines play a significant role in achieving the source code quality. The standard guidelines to be followed to develop quality code are as follows:

- Naming Conventions: Some of the naming conventions are as follows:
    - Global variables should start with an uppercase letter
    - Local variables should generally be nouns starting with lowercase
    - Constant names should be in uppercase
    - Package names should be in lowercase
    - Methods and functions should be verbs starting with lowercase
    - Avoid long variable names

- Comments: Comments are descriptive statements that help the reader to understand the code. For better readability, the comments should be specified for each module or function in the code. Each programming language has a comment delimiter that can be used to provide the text for better clarity.

- Standard headers: A common header has to be followed for all the modules in the program. This may include the name of the module, the author's name, the date on which the module is created, the date of the last modification, different functions of the module, etc.

- Use of Globals: The global variables have to be identified with utmost care and a limit to use.

- Coding guidelines
    - The code should be easy to understand. Develop a code that is easy to understand. This makes debugging and maintenance difficult.
    - Avoid long functions and methods: A long code is difficult to understand, reuse and maintain. Hence a method generally should not exceed 10-15 lines of code.
    - Proper comments are required at least for every block of code.
    - The source code should be properly indented for better understanding, clarity, and debugging.
    - Variable names should be meaningful for better understandability.
    - Avoid Go To statements as they make the program unstructured.
    - Properly manage side effects: Changes in global variables may make understanding the code complex. Further, it will be not be easy to maintain.
    - Avoid complex conditional expressions.

Code review starts once a module is successfully compiled. Code reviews help eliminate coding errors and aim to produce high-quality code. Code review is generally carried out when the module is free from syntax errors. The two types of code review techniques are code walkthrough and code inspection.

In the code walkthrough, a module is taken for review by development team members. Each member tests a module with several test cases. The objective of the code walkthrough is to detect any logical errors in the source code. Each member notes their observation and discusses the same in the walkthrough meeting. Based on members' observations, the code is modified, tested for syntax errors, and submitted for a code walkthrough. This process is repeated till the walkthrough team is satisfied with the source code.

In code inspection, the source code is checked for common errors that are in the code due to the oversight of the programmer. It may also check whether coding standards and guidelines have been followed. The code inspection is generally carried out by an expert who will be able to identify the common errors. The experts will identify the errors, and the source code will be modified accordingly.

UNIT SUMMARY

- ***Design Principles***
    - *Problem Decomposition and Hierarchy*
    - *Abstraction*
    - *Modularity*
- ***Modular Design***
    - *Coupling*
    - *Cohesion*
- ***Software Architecture***
- ***Architectural Styles***
    - *Model-View-Controller Architecture*
    - *Layered Architecture*
    - *Repository Architecture*
    - *Client-Server Architecture*
    - *Pipe and Filter Architecture*
- ***User Interface Design***
    - *User Interface Design Process*
    - *User Interface Design Principles*
- ***Object Oriented Design***
    - *Interaction Diagram*
    - *Class Diagram*
    - *Case Study: Object Oriented Design*
- ***Stuctured System Design***
    - *Structure Chart*
    - *Tranform Analysis*
    - *Transaction Analysis*
- ***Coding Principles***

EXERCISES

Multiple Choice Questions

3.1 The process in which only essential details are specified without giving inner-level details is

(a) Abstraction (b) Hierarchy (c) Partitioning (d) Detailed design

3.2 The strength of the relationship between the modules of a system is

(a) Cohesion (b) Abstraction (c) Coupling (d) Architecture

3.3 In one of the following architectures, shared data is used across the applications

(a) MVC (b) Repository (c) Pipe and Filter (d) Cloud

3.4 One of the diagrams is used to model the interaction of time ordering of messages between the objects

(a) Class diagram
(b) Collaboration diagram
(c) Communication diagram
(d) Sequence diagram

3.5 The notation that is used to destroy an object dynamically in an interaction diagram is

(a) Del (b) X (c) ! (d) &

3.6 The software design artifact of structured system design is a

(a) Class diagram (b) Sequence diagram
(c) Collaboration diagram (d) Structure Chart

3.7 In one of the following methods, the structure chart is divided into input, process, and output modules

(a) Transform Analysis (b) Transaction Analysis
(c) Object-oriented design (d) None of the above

3.8 The cohesion that exists between functions of a module when the output of one function becomes an input to the other is

(a) Functional (b) Sequential
(c) Procedural (d) Communicational

3.9 When the modules of the system commmunicate using composite data structures that it said to be

(a) Common Coupling (b) Control Coupling
(c) Stamp Coupling (d) Data Coupling

3.10 The most desirable form of coupling is

(a) Data coupling (b) Control coupling
(c) Common coupling (d) Stamp coupling

Answers of Multiple Choice Questions
3.1 (a), 3.2(c), 3.3(b), 3.4(d), 3.5(b), 3.6(d), 3.7(a), 3.8 (a), 3.9(c), 3.10 (a)

Short and Long Answer Type Questions

3.1 Differentiate between analysis and design

3.2 What are design principles? How do you evaluate the design?

3.3 Differentiate between (i) Coupling and Cohesion (ii) Functional and Data Abstraction Requirements (iii) Object-oriented design and Structured design.

3.4 What is modularity? Why is it required

3.5 What are design principles? What issues emerge if the design principles are not followed

3.6 Specify different scenarios that help in achieving loose coupling and tight cohesion

3.7 Propose a software architecture when the following characteristics are critical to the system's development (i) Security and Availability (ii) Maintainability and Performance (iii) Maintianability and Availability

3.8 What are user interface design principles? Why are they required for a user interface design?

3.9 Differentiate between (i) Object Oriented and Structured System design (ii) Sequence and Collaboration diagram

3.10 What is a class diagram? How is it modeled

3.11 Describe the relationships used in modeling class diagrams along with their notations. Give Examples.

3.12 What is transform analysis? Explain the procedure to convert a data flow diagram into a structure chart using transform analysis.

PRACTICAL

3.1 Consider any program or an application you have developed and identify various types of coupling and cohesion in it.

3.2 Suggest suitable architectures for the given applications considering combinations of various quality charcteristics (non-functional requirements)
(a) Banking System (b) Railway reservation System (c) Online Shopping System

3.3 Design the given applications using object oriented design and structured design (a) Railway reservation System (b) Online Shopping System.

3.4 Model any project using the appropriate design paradigms and convert it into source code by selecting target programming language.

KNOW MORE

Software design helps in realizing the solution for the problems stated by the customer. The first step in the software design process is to decide the system's architecture. The system's structure is modeled based on the non-functional or quality characteristics of the target system. However, well-defined architectural patterns can be used if it suits the solution domain.

In the next step, the software design paradigm is decided based on the target environment in which the system will be implemented. Accordingly, object-oriented or structured design is adopted. An effective user interface design is required so the system user can access its features easily, thus satisfying the usability characteristics.

If the object-oriented design is adopted, the use cases that are identified during the requirements analysis phase are realized. The use case is realized by modeling each scenario using interaction diagrams. The interaction diagrams show the exchange of messages between the objects. Then a class diagram is modeled. In some systems, it is evident that some of the objects change their state based on certain events. In such a case, a state transition diagram has to be modeled. A state transition diagram consists of states that define objects' characteristics and transitions that change an object from one state to another. The transition happens when an event occurs. An event can be a call, event, or time event. Once an event occurs, the appropriate method is invoked, which changes the state of the object. The state transition diagrams can also model the guard condition. *Guard condition* is a boolean expression that must be true for triggering an event. The artifacts of state transition diagrams help in realizing event-driven systems.

The data flow diagrams are converted to a structure chart if the structured design is adopted. DFD will be converted to a structure chart depending on the type of systems, transform, or transaction-driven systems.

The design artifacts are then converted to source code. The source code has to be written by following specific standards and guidelines. The source code is tested for syntax errors and will go through the code review process. In the code review process, the source code is corrected before it goes through the formal testing.

If source code is given and one wants to know the working of a system, then the design should be available. The process of converting source code to design is said to be reverse engineering.

REFERENCES AND SUGGESTED READINGS

- Sommerville, I. (2016) Software Engineering. 10th Edition, Pearson Education Limited, Boston

- Roger S. Pressman (2010) Software Engineering: A Practitioner's Approach, McGraw-Hill

- Rajib Mall (2018), Fundamentals of Software Engineering, 5th Edition, PHI Learning Private Limited.

- Pankaj Jalote (2010), Software Engineering: A Precise Approach, Wiley-India

- Grady Booch, James Rumbaugh, Ivar Jacobson (2017), The Unified Modeling Language User Guide, 2nd Edition, Pearson India Education Services Pvt. Ltd.

- IEEE Recommended Practice for Software Design Descriptions (1016-1998)

Dynamic QR Code for Further Reading

4 Software Testing

UNIT SPECIFICS

Through this unit we have discussed the following aspects:

- *Testing Concepts;*
- *Testing process;*
- *Functional testing;*
- *Structural testing;*
- *Levels of testing;*
- *Quality Assurance;*

The practical applications of the topics are discussed for generating further curiosity and creativity as well as improving problem solving capacity.

Besides giving multiple choice questions as well as questions of short and long answer types marked in two categories following lower and higher order of Bloom's taxonomy, assignments, a list of references and suggested readings are given in the unit so that one can go through them for practice. It is important to note that for getting more information on various topics of interest some QR codes have been provided in different sections which can be scanned for relevant supportive knowledge.

After the related practical, based on the content, there is a "Know More" section. This section has been carefully designed so that the supplementary information provided in this part becomes beneficial for the users of the book. This section mainly highlights the initial activity, examples of some interesting facts, analogy, history of the development of the subject focusing the salient observations and finding, timelines starting from the development of the concerned topics up to the recent time, applications of the subject matter for our day-to-day real life or/and industrial applications on variety of aspects, case study related to environmental, sustainability, social and ethical issues whichever applicable, and finally inquisitiveness and curiosity topics of the unit.

RATIONALE

One of the issues with software development is that the delivered system often fails to meet the customer's expectations. One of the reasons for this is improper and unbiased testing in software development phases. Testing is the process of verifying whether the behavior of the software or a program is as per the user's expectations. Testing is generally used to test the source code. However, testing is required at each phase of development. The specifications must be tested to check whether they meet the customer's requirements.

Similarly, the design must be tested to determine whether it meets the requirements specifications. The errors can occur at any stage of software development. If the source code does not give the expected outcome, then the program's internal structure has to be tested to identify the bugs in the system.

Testing is an important activity that requires significant effort. A systematic approach to software testing is required to produce better-quality software. Testing aims to detect errors, and the process of fixing these errors is said to be debugging.

Quality software is the one which is compliant with the user's requirements. The user requirements are the expected features of the system. For each expected behavior, there is a need to define a set of test cases. The test cases are used to examine the actual behavior of the system. If the expected and actual behavior matches, then the test case is said to be passed. Otherwise, there is a defect in a particular test case. The development team then rectifies the errors, and the testing is again performed. There is a need to follow a testing process that includes test planning, test design, test execution, test reports, and closure.

Testing cannot be exhaustive. It is challenging to test a program with all possible inputs. Further, it is difficult to say when the testing will end. In addition to testing the system's functionality, the software has to be tested for performance, reliability, maintainability, usability, etc., depending on the system's desired non-functional characteristics. The developers generally try to prove that the software works correctly. To avoid any bias, it is preferred that the testing need to be carried out by the testing team, which is different from the development team. Test reports are the primary artifacts of testing activity.

As testing is a challenging task, it is sometimes difficult to understand why a defect occurs. The solution is first to test the simple functions, and then the functions are integrated to check the correctness of a module. In the next step, the modules are integrated to test the entire system. The interfaces are to be tested during the integration activity. Tests are initially realized using artificial data. Before delivering the system to the customer, the system has to be tested with actual data by the customer. Quality control is the process of detecting and correcting a defect, whereas quality assurance is the process of defect prevention.

PRE-REQUISITES

Computer Programming (Diploma Semester-III)

Scripting Languages (Diploma Semester-III)

UNIT OUTCOMES

List of outcomes of this unit is as follows:

U4-O4: Understand the software testing fundamentals

U4-O4: Understand and apply black box testing techniques

U4-O4 : Understand and apply white box testing techniques

U4-O4: Understand the levels of testing.

U4-O4: Understand the quality assurance process

Unit-4 Outcomes	EXPECTED MAPPING WITH COURSE OUTCOMES (1- Weak Correlation; 2- Medium correlation; 3- Strong Correlation)				
	CO-1	CO-2	CO-3	CO-4	CO-5
U4-O1	1	1	1	1	3
U4-O2	1	2	2	2	3
U4-O3	1	2	2	2	3
U4-O4	1	1	2	2	3
U4- O5	1	2	3	3	3

4.1 TESTING PRELIMINARIES

Software design aims at testing an application to find errors. The testing process is realized in each phase of software development. Even after testing a program sufficiently, it cannot be guaranteed that the program is error-free. It is not possible to exhaustively test any program or software with all possible inputs. If the program doesn't behave as expected, then the instance of the failure is noted, which will be rectified during the debugging process.

4.1.1 Error, Fault and Failure

According to IEEE std.1044-2009,An error is a human action that produces an incorrect result. Error or defect generally occurs when the development team fails to understand the functionality properly and is not able to transform the design into source code appropriately. An error may lead to a fault. The system that has yet to produce the expected output might be because of improper implementation of functionality or its parts.

The condition that causes a program not to exhibit its expected behavior is said to be a *fault* or bug. The fault generally occurs when the program or software doesn't include the mechanisms to handle abnormal behavior in the program. This includes a lack of fault tolerance in the source code, inappropriate data, lack of resources, etc. Conditions like the inability to handle divide-by-zero errors and the reading of unavailable data also lead to faults. If a fault is not managed, it may lead to failures. Faults can be prevented by following coding principles and guidelines. Faults can be addressed by implementing code review techniques like walkthroughs and inspections.

Failure is the inability of a program to meet its functionality. This makes the system unresponsive. If the end user detects an issue in the product, it is referred to as a failure, as the software cannot perform the required functionalities. The accumulation of several defects also leads to failure. Failure exists when faults are present in the system. Failures may be caused by the inability to realize the system's functional or non-functional requirements. In some systems, the functionality is implemented successfully, but it does not satisfy the desired non-functional characteristics, leading to failures.

A safety-critical system is one whose failure may result in severe damage or loss to the environment, life, or equipment. If the automated surgery system can perform the surgery but cannot complete the process within the stipulated time, it may lead to failures.

4.1.2. Test Oracle

A Test oracle is a mechanism to determine whether the actual behavior confirms the system's expected. Test oracle (Fig 4.1) is used to check the correctness of the outcome of software or a program. In the testing process, the test cases are given to test oracle and the software under testing. The output of the test oracle (expected behavior) is compared with the output of the software under test to check the correctness of the system.

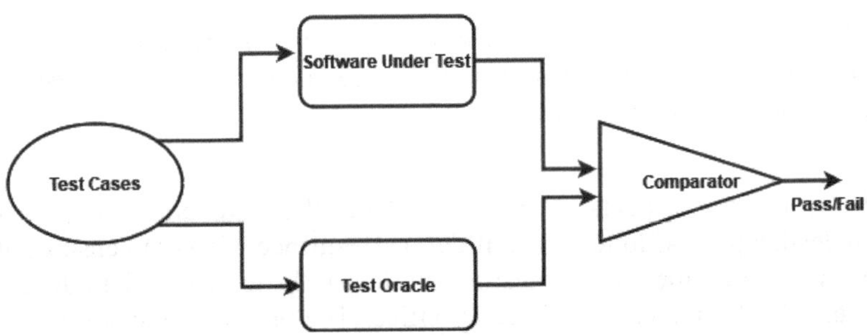

Fig. 4.1: Test Oracle

Test oracles are required to realize testing activity. Generally, the oracles are human beings, which may lead to several mistakes. There can be a discrepancy between the software and test Oracle results. Hence there is a need to automate the test oracles, which are generated from programs, specifications, etc. The programs, specifications, and other artifacts are expected to be complete, consistent, and unambiguous. Test oracles can also be used to test the system's specification, architecture, and design.

4.1.3. Verification and Validation

Verification is determining whether the output produced in one phase of software development confirms the conditions stated at the beginning of that phase. In contrast, validation determines whether the total system confirms the requirements stated at the beginning of the project. Verification is required after each phase of software development. However, validation is done once the final product is available.

Verification is the process of testing a system in a simulated environment, whereas validation is the process of testing a system in a live environment. If the *verification* is *diligently* carried out at the end of each phase, then validation would be simple. Testing includes both verification and validation activity. Inspection, reviews, and walkthroughs are used for verification, whereas testing of the end product is done for validation.

According to Boehm,
Verification: "Are we building the right product?"
Validation: "Are we building the product right?"

Testing whether the requirements specification is as per the requirements given by the customer is verification. Testing whether the design produced confirms the software requirements specification document is verification. Testing whether the module or a function confirms the design is verification. Testing the final software deliverable to check whether it meets the customer's requirements is validation.

4.2 TESTING PROCESS

ANSI/IEEE 1059 standard defines *software testing* as "The process of analyzing a software item to detect the differences between existing and required conditions (defects/errors/bugs) and to evaluate the features of the software item."

In order to test the artifacts of software effectively, a systematic approach is required. The software testing process follows a well-defined sequence of tasks to ensure software quality. The testing team defines the scope of testing. Various tasks to be tested are listed, and the entry and exit criteria for testing each task are specified. The phases in the software testing process are specified in Figure 4.2.

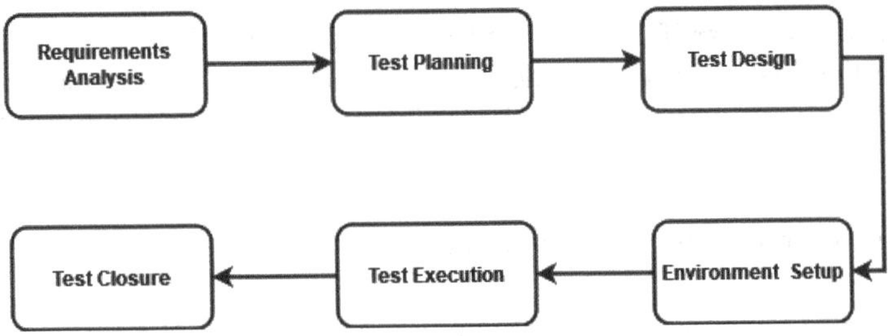

Fig. 4.2: Testing Process

4.2.1 Requirements Analysis

The testing team needs to understand the requirements to test the system effectively. The testing team reviews the requirements specification document to identify the scope of testing. The test engineers will meet the other teams to identify the test tasks. A list of tests for testing functionality, performance, security, and other requirements is prepared.

In section 2.3.2 (Indian Bank case study), three use cases were identified: Deposit, withdrawal, and transfer. These are the functional requirements to be tested. The use case specification specifies the tasks in each of these use cases. Similarly, the university library case study (section 2.3.4) specifies several functions to realize the issue and return book functionalities.

4.2.2 Test Planning

The resources and workforce required to test a system are planned in this phase. The testing deliverables are defined. The effort and cost required to perform testing are estimated. The schedule of testing various artifacts is also decided. Roles and responsibilities are assigned to the testing team.

The effort, schedule, and workforce required to test various functionalities must be estimated. Furthermore, this phase also plans whether the testing should be done manually or using automated tools.

4.2.3 Test Design

In this phase, the test cases are designed. The test scenarios and the test data for each scenario are created. The expected outputs of each test case are also listed.

A test case is a triplet <I, S, O>. Where I is the set of input data given to the system, S is the system's state, and O is the output or outcome produced by the system. The state represents software development artifacts produced at the end of each phase. A test suite is a set of test cases with which the quality of a given deliverable is tested. A system may consist of different test suites. Each test suite may represent the testing of a module or functionality which requires a set of test cases.

The guidelines for test case design are as follows:

- Select inputs so that the system or module generates errors.
- Design test cases that cause input buffers to overflow
- Force the system to generate invalid outputs.
- Give inputs such that the computational results are too large or too small.

Test First Development (TFD) prepares test cases before the system is implemented. Generally, the agile development process follows the TFD approach, where the user is also involved in deciding the test cases. Once the sprint is ready, it is tested with the test suite, which was designed before realizing the story. Furthermore, pair programming also helps test the system better, where one member writes a program and the other reviews it to suggest any changes. This verification process helps in developing better systems.

For example, each use case (section 2.3.2) has a set of tasks specified in the use case specification. Test cases are written for each of the tasks. The test cases for all use case tasks form a test suite. The generic format of a test case is given in Fig. 4.3.of a use case forms a test suite. The generic format of a test case is given in Fig. 4.3.

Test id	Tasks	Expected Result	Actual Result	Status
				Pass/Fail

Fig. 4.3: Test Design template

Each test case has a test id, and the task or test case description specifies the functionality to be tested. The Expected result of each task is specified.

4.2.4 Environment Setup

The essential software and hardware are required to create a test environment. A list of required software and hardware is prepared. For automated testing, the required testing tools are identified. This activity can be done in parallel with the test design phase.

4.2.5 Test Execution

During this phase, the testing team tests the software's features using the test cases. Test execution, process, refers to the execution of a set of programs or functions for the given set of inputs. The expected results are compared with the actual results produced. Any defects identified during test execution are recorded. The severity level of the defect reported is also recorded so that the development team can prioritize the issues to be addressed. This phase is iterated after the development team has removed the defects. The success or failure of test cases is updated in the test reports. Once a task is tested, the actual results and the status of the testing activity are updated in Fig. 4.3.

4.2.6 Test Closure

Test closure is the final step in software testing. It is to ensure that all testing activities are completed and documented. The feedback from the entire testing process is collected. In the next testing life cycle, feedback is used to improve the testing process.

4.3 BLACK BOX TESTING

The black box or functional testing involves testing a system, module, or function without knowing its design or the source code. The test engineer knows the inputs and expected outputs and is unaware of how the inputs are transformed into respective outputs.

The following are the guidelines for black box testing:

- Identify the functionality to be tested. Understand its scope and objectives
- Identify the resources required for testing functionality.
- Create a test suite containing test cases to test the functionality and list the expected outcome
- Execute the test cases and record the outcome of the test (Successful/Unsuccessful)
- Submit the report to the development team
- Repeat the process for all functions and modules of the software.

Testing a system with all possible inputs is an impractical exhaustive test. For example, to compute the roots of the quadratic equation $ax^2+bx+c=0$, we need three inputs a, b and c. If all three variables occupy 2 bytes, we need a total of $2^{16}*2^{16}*2^{16}=2^{48}$ test cases to test the program with all possible inputs.

The essential criteria for the black box testing technique is to design the appropriate test cases to test the system sufficiently. Several black box techniques will help in designing the test cases. Each testing method has its pros and cons. However, some bugs can't be detected by any of the methods.

4.3.1 Equivalence Class Partitioning

As exhaustive testing is impractical, in equivalence class partitioning or equivalence partitioning method, the input domain is divided into a finite number of classes or groups based on the similarity in the resultant outcome, which is a partition. It is assumed that if the representatives from each group or class produce an outcome, all the elements from the same group also produce the same outcome. If one test case in a group or class results in an error, then all the test cases of the same class are also expected to produce the same error. Since all values in a partition are expected to produce the same output, they are equivalent partitions. The equivalent partitions are to be made both for valid and invalid inputs. This method is used to reduce the total number of test cases to a finite set of test cases and satisfy the behavior of the entire input domain.

There are two steps to performing testing using equivalence partitioning. First, identify all partitions from the input and output values for the software under test. Secondly, test each partition with one member to maximize the complete coverage.

Enter Marks (between 0 to 100) :

Equivalence Class Partitioning		
Invalid	**Valid**	**Invalid**
<0	0-100	>100

Fig. 4.4: Equivalence Class Partitioning scenario

In Fig. 4.4, the system's user has to enter input (marks). The valid range of marks is between 0-100. Suppose the value entered by the user is between 0-100; it is a valid input. If the output produced is correct for any value between 0-100, it is assumed that the same output will be produced for all values between 0-100. The other two equivalence classes are for invalid inputs. In one of them, the input is a negative number, and in another class, the input is greater than 100.

4.3.2 Boundary Value Analysis

It is observed that frequent errors are committed by programmers while dealing with boundary conditions. The boundary condition refers to the input value, which is around the limits of values. If variable X's input domain is between 1 to 100, then the test cases for boundary values include 0,1,2,99,100,101.

Boundary value analysis (BVA) is an approach to finding defects at the boundaries. One of the reasons for the occurrence of such defects is that the programmers may misuse the relation operators. For example, they may use > instead of >= or < instead of <=. The boundary value analysis technique will help in identifying those defects. The second reason for such defects is the confusion caused by implementing several iterative constructs. Each of these may have different terminating conditions. For example, the condition used in a while may differ in do..while for all scenarios. The third reason for such defects is an improper understanding of the requirements.

The software testing life cycle's defect design phase must identify all such conditional statements and loops to incorporate test cases for boundary value analysis. Boundary value analysis can also be used in white box testing to check internal data structures' boundary or limit conditions like stacks, queues, and arrays.

Consider an example where the range $0 \leq X \leq 10$ has to be tested. The test cases include 0,1, 9,10 (valid inputs), and -1,11 (invalid inputs). If each input has a defined range (first, last), the six boundary values are first-1, first, first+1, last-1, last, and last+1.

4.3.3 Decision Table

Decision table technique is used when there are several actions taken based on the combinations of conditions based on the inputs given to the system. It is used to analyse the complex logical relationship between several elements of the system. The general form of decision table is specified in Fig. 4.5.

		Conditional Entries			
Conditional Statements	C_1	True	True	False	False
	C_2	True	True	False	True
	C_3	True	False	True	False
		Action Entries			
Action Statements	A_1	√			
	A_2			√	
	A_3		√		
	A_4				√

Fig. 4.5: Decision Table

The decision table consists of four quadrants: Conditional Statements, Conditional Entries, Action Statements, and Action Entries. The Conditional statements specify the individual boolean conditions ($C_1..C_m$). As per the requirements, the possible truth values are specified in the conditional entries section. The possible actions ($A_1.. A_n$) to be realized are specified in Action Statements section. The action based on the conditional entries is specified in the Action Entries section.

For example, a bank provides interest rates for female senior citizens at 11%, male senior citizens at 10%, and for the rest of the customers, it is at 8%. The decision table for the given scenario is given in Fig 4.6.

		Conditional Entries			
Conditional Statements	C_1- Female	False	False	True	True
	C_2- Senior Citizen	False	True	False	True
		Action Entries			
Action Statements	A1- Interest-11%				√
	A_2 - Interest-10%		√		
	A_3 - Interest-8%	√		√	

Fig. 4.6: Decision Table for interest rate computation

4.3.4 Cause Effect Graph

Unlike equivalence class partitioning and boundary value analysis, a cause-Effect graph is a technique that considers the combination of input conditions so that the test cases become manageable and provide clarity to test the outcome of an artifact under test. Causes and effects are find identified for the system under test. A cause and effect represent distinct conditions and outcomes of the system or program under testing.

Each condition(cause) is represented as a node. The output produced is terminal action nodes called Effects. Conditions are combined using intermediate nodes or boolean operators that result in an effect in the cause-effect graph.

Consider the condition and action statements specified in Fig. 4.6. The conditions are C1- Female, C2- Senior Citizen, and effects are E1- Interest 11%, E2- Interest 10%, and E3- Interest 8%. The cause-effect graph of the given scenario is specified in Fig. 4.7.

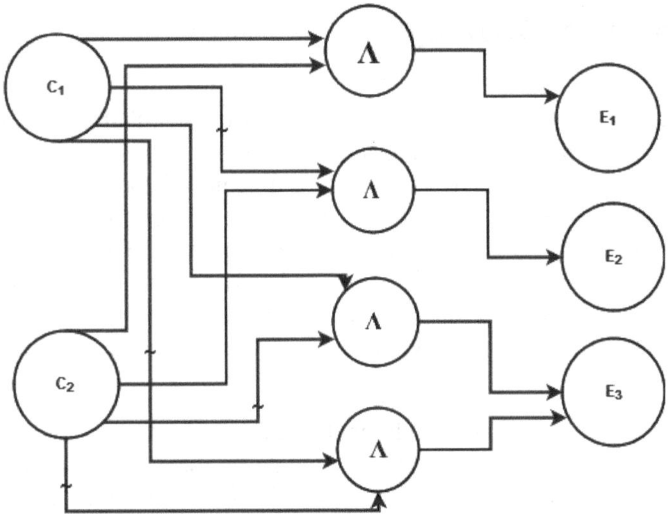

Fig. 4.7: Cause-Effect Graph

From the above figure, the following test cases are derived:

$C_1 \wedge C_2 \rightarrow E_1$ //For given inputs if C_1 and C_2 are true, then the output is E_1

$\neg C_1 \wedge C_2 \rightarrow E_2$ //For given inputs if C_1 is false and C_2 is true, then the output is E_2

$C_1 \wedge \neg C_2 \rightarrow E_3$ //For given inputs if C_1 is true and C_2 is false, then the output is E_3

$\neg C_1 \wedge \neg C_2 \rightarrow E_3$ //For given inputs if C_1 and C_2 are false, then the output is E_3

4.4 WHITE BOX TESTING

The black box testing is used to test the functionality of the system. This is done to check whether the system with given inputs gives the expected outcome. It does not deal with the internal structure of the program. White box testing, structural testing, or glass box testing checks the program's internal logic. The test cases are designed to check the program logic. The developers of the system do this. White box testing considers the program structure and internal design flow. Generally, the defects in the program under test are developed due to incorrect translation of design into a source code. Other defects are caused by programmers or by programming language constructs used.

White box testing uses test cases to test the various criteria in the program structure. *Code coverage* is a glass box testing technique that verifies how much code is executed. It involves test case design and execution to determine the percentage of the source code covered by the testing. Code coverage testing includes a statement, condition, path, and function coverage.

4.4.1 Statement Coverage

Statement coverage refers to designing the test cases such that each statement in the program is executed at least once. The statements in a program can be simple, compound, conditional, or iterative. The code coverage is expected to be achieved for each type of statement. The code consisting of statements (other than conditional or iterative statements) that are executed sequentially generally starts at the first statement and will go through all statements until the last statement is reached. It appears that 100% code coverage is achieved in this scenario. However, if these statements produce abnormal behavior or exceptions such as divide-by-zero, then if a test case starts at the beginning may not cover all statements in the program.

When the statement is a simple conditional statement like if..then..else, there should be a test case for if.. then part and else part of the conditional statement. The test cases should be designed so that each part of conditional statements is tested at least once. Similarly, the nested..if and switch statements would require multiple test cases for each conditional statement in if..else ladder and for each case in the switch statement.

An iterative statement executes a set of statements repeatedly until or while a certain boolean condition is satisfied. Loops may fail because of improper handling of boundary conditions in the boolean condition. The improper termination condition may also be the cause of the defect. For better coverage of iterative statements, a loop need to be tested around the boundary. Further loop need to be tested for normal operations when the condition is true and otherwise.

*Statement coverage = (Total statements executed/Total number of executable statements) * 100*

The number of test cases increases from simple statements to conditional and iterative statements. However, exhaustive coverage of all statements is impractical. Further, even if the program has high statement coverage, the software under test will not be defect free. Consider the source code in Fig. 4.8.

```
Oddeven(int n){
    if (n%2==0)
        pr intf("Even");
    else
        printf("Odd");
}
```

Fig. 4.8: oddeven() function

The two scenarios for computing statement coverage of the oddeven() function is given in Figure 4.9.

Scenario-1 (n=12)	Scenario-2 (n=15)
1. Oddeven(int n) { 2. if (n%2==0) 3. printf("Even"); 4. else 5. printf("Odd"); 6. }	1. Oddeven(int n) { 2. if (n%2==0) 3. printf("Even"); 4. else 5. printf("Odd"); 6. }
Statement coverage= (4/6) *100= 66.67%	Statement coverage = (5/6) *100= 83.33%

Fig. 4.9: Statement coverage for two scenarios of Oddeven() function

Both scenarios cover all statements. Hence the code coverage is 100%.

Consider the source code given in Fig. 4.10

```
sample(int n){
        int p;
         m=0;
        if (n%2==0)
          m=m+n;
          n++;
        else
          p=n/m
      }
```

Fig. 4.10: Sample function for statement coverage

The two scenarios for computing statement coverage of the sample() function (Fig. 4.10) is given in Figure 4.11.

Scenario-1 (n=2)	Scenario-2 (n=3)
sample(int n){	sample(int n){
int p;	int p;
m=0;	m=0;
if (n%2==0){	if (n%2==0){
m=m+n;	m=m+n;
n++; }	n++;
else	else
p=n/m;	p=n/m;
}	}
Statement coverage= (7/9) *100= 77.78%	Program fails

Fig. 4.11: Statement coverage for two scenarios of sample() function

In the above program, if the function is tested with an even n value, we will get 77.78% of code coverage. However, if the value entered is odd, the program often fails (because of the divide-by-zero error). Even though the code coverage is 77.78% when the number is even but the program may fail the majority of times if the inputs to the function are odd most of the time. The statement coverage cant be decided only by checking one condition.

4.4.2 Condition Coverage

Condition coverage is a white box testing technique used to test both possible results of a predicate and different combinations of predicates or conditions in compound boolean expressions. The test cases should be defined so that each condition has to be evaluated for various combinations of each elementary condition.

Condition coverage =

*(Total decisions executed / Total number of decisions statements in the program) * 100*

Consider the simple program segement given in Fig. 4.12

```
myfunc( ){
        int a=10;
        if (a>=10)
          printf("Valid input");
        else
          printf ("Invalid input");
          }
```

Fig. 4.12: Sample function for condition coverage

The test suite for the condition coverage of Fig 4.12 is given in Fig. 4.13

Test case	a>=10	Output
1	True	Valid input
2	False	Invalid input

Fig. 4.13: Condition coverage for Fig. 4.12

Consider the program segment given in Figure 4.14

```
func(int p, int q, int r, int s){
        if ((p==0 || q==0) && (r+s)>=2))
          printf("Welcome");
        else
                printf ("Thank you");
        }
```

Fig. 4.14: Program with compound condition

The program segment of Fig. 4.14 requires a test suite to satisfy the compound condition criterion. The condition(p==0 || q==0) involves a logical OR operator. If p=0, the value is True for the first condition. As the logical OR operator is used, the predicate (q==0) need not be checked. This can be combined with both values of True and False outcome of the third condition. The test case required to adequately check a predicate or condition is 2^n, where n is the number of conditions. This would be impractical for the programs with many conditions. However, short circuit evaluation may reduce the number of test cases. The test cases for the condition coverage of Fig. 4.14 are given in Fig. 4.15.

Test case	p==0	q==0	(r + s)>=2	Output
1	True	Don't care	False	Thank you
2	True	Don't care	True	Welcome
3	False	True	False	Thank you
4	False	True	True	Welcome
5	False	False	Not required	Thank you

Fig. 4.15: Condition coverage of Fig. 4.14

In test case-1, test case-2, and test case-5, only two conditions are checked. All three conditions are checked in test case-3 and test case-4, respectively. The drawback of this approach is that as the conditional statements increase, it will be impractical to carry out exhaustive testing for conditional coverage.

4.4.3 Path Coverage

Path coverage is a white box testing technique where test cases are designed to test all possible paths in a program from the beginning to the end. The test cases should be designed so that each of the paths in the program is tested. The number of linearly independent paths in the program can be computed using a cyclomatic complexity measure.

A program or a module can be represented as a flow graph, a directed graph where the vertex represents a statement or a block and the edge represents the control flow. V_i and V_j are vertices of a program; an edge from node V_i to V_j means the statement V_j is executed immediately after the execution of statement V_i. Let N be the number of vertices, E the number of edges, and P the connected components of a flow graph. Then the cyclomatic complexity is computed as

$$V(G) = E - N + P.$$

The cyclomatic complexity that represents the number of independent paths in the given program is also expressed as

$$V(G) = N(DE) + 1$$

Where N(DE) is the number of Decision Elements (conditions) in the program.

Consider the program given in Fig. 4.16.

```
1.  Perfectn( int n)
2.  {
3.      int  sum=0, i, k=1;
4.      while (k<=n)
5.      {
6.          for(i=1; i<=k/2; i++)
7.          {
8.              if (k%i==0)
9.                  sum=sum + i;
10.         }
11.         if (sum==k)
12.             printf("%d  ",k);
13.         k++;
14.         sum=0;
15.     }
16. }
```

Fig. 4.16: Function to display perfect numbers upto n

The flow graph of the program (Fig 4.16) is given in Fig. 4.17

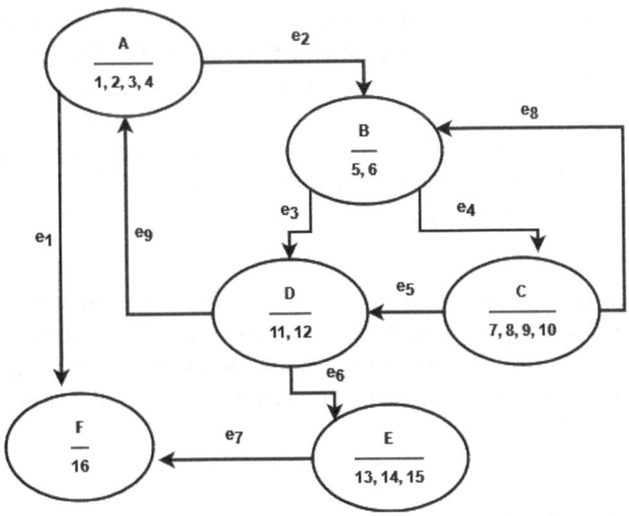

Fig. 4.17: Control Flow graph for Fig. 4.16

In Fig 4.17, there are six vertices and nine edges. The vertex A consists of statements 1,2,3,4. Once a program starts, these four statements are executed. Then, separate flows are realized based on the decision taken in statement 5.

The cyclomatic complexity of the graph is V(G) = 9-6+2 = 5

The number of Decision elements in the program (statement-4,6,8,11) is 4. The cyclomatic complexity V(G) = 4+1 =5.

There are five linearly independent Paths in the program.

Path-1: A-F

Path-2: A-B-D-E-F

Path-3: A-B-D-A-B-D-E-F

Path-4: A-B-C-D-E-F

Path-5: A-B-C-B-C-D-E-F

The test cases are to be written to test all paths in the program. For a given test suite, the path coverage is defined as

Path coverage =

*(Total paths executed / Total number of paths in the program) * 100*

4.4.4 Function coverage

Function coverage is a white box testing used to determine how many functions the test cases cover. The requirements are mapped into the functions in the design phase. For example, the data flow diagrams are converted to structure charts in structured systems. In function coverage, the test cases are to be written for different functions to check the correctness of the functionality. The data and control couple information provided in structure charts also help know the inputs and expected outputs from the function at the low levels. This also helps test whether the code written is as per the design produced.

There are several advantages of function coverage. It is easier to test a function as it will be easier to check if the function produces the desired output. If not, the functionality has to be modified. Further, we can also measure the number of calls to the function. If they are excessive calls, they can be optimized. Not all functions can be tested at a time. For a given test suite, the function coverage is defined as

Function coverage =

*(Total functions executed / Total number of functions in the program) * 100*

4.5 LEVELS OF TESTING

Developers and test engineers cannot test any application in a single go, as detecting bugs in a monolithic program will be difficult. There are several tests to be carried out for testing an application. There are four stages of development testing.

- Unit testing
- Integration testing
- System testing
- Acceptance testing

Testing levels are specified in Fig. 4.18. Unit testing is generally referred to as testing in the small as individual units are tested, whereas integration and system testing are termed as testing in the large.

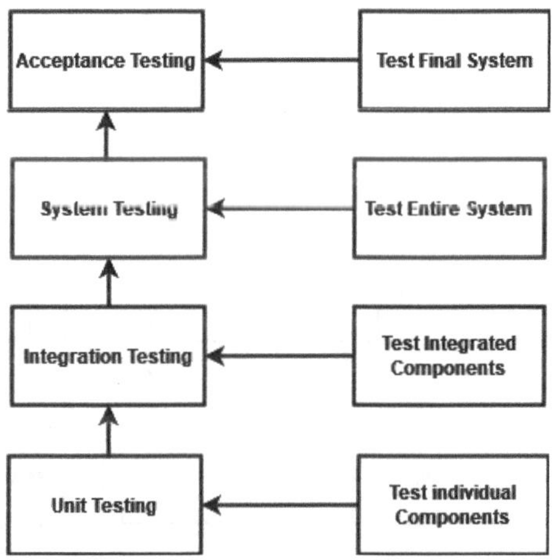

Fig. 4.18: Levels of Testing

4.5.1 Unit Testing

Once the coding of a module or a component is complete, it has to be tested for its correctness. Unit testing is the process of testing individual modules or components. The developers do it. The test cases for testing a module or a component need to be designed, and the test environment is to be made ready to perform the unit testing.

The source code must be available to test a single function or module. Additionally, the non-local or shared data structure that the module accesses is to be made available. A module can call or is called by another module. If a module has to call another module, then it is required that the called module has to be tested first. If a program consists of several functions, then each function is tested as a part of unit testing.

4.5.2 Integration Testing

Once the individual modules are tested, the modules or components of the system are tested together as all units work together to realize the system's functionality. Integration testing aims to find defects that arise from the combination of various functional units. Integration generally refers to interactions between various units or modules of the system. The interactions which are modeled as interfaces between modules need to be tested. Integration testing focuses on testing the interfaces between the modules of the system.

All modules may not be available to perform integration testing. However, to continue the testing activity, dummy modules simulating similar functionality are used for integration. Consider the set of units of a system and their interactions given in Fig. 4.19.

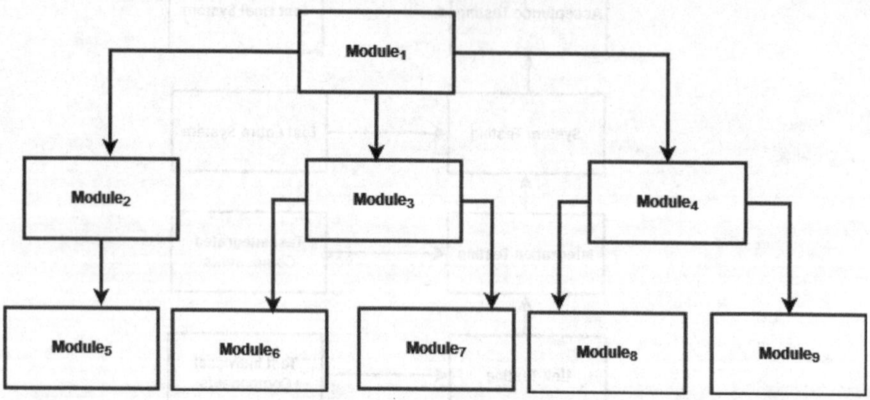

Fig. 4.19: Modules and interfaces

It is evident from the above figure that there are nine modules. Each module is separately tested in unit testing. The solid line specifies the explicit interactions between the modules. There are a total of 8 explicit interfaces which need to be tested. The methods for integration are as follows:

- Top-down integration
- Bottom-up integration
- Sandwich or Bi-directional integration
- Big-Bang integration

In top-down integration, testing involves the topmost module or unit interfacing with other units at the next level in the same order to cover all components. Consider the modularization of Fig 4.19. In top-down integration the integration starts with $Module_1$ and $Module_2$. The order in which interfaces are tested in top-down integration is given in Fig 4.20.

Step	Interfaces to be tested
1	1-2
2	1-3
3	1-4
4	1-2-5
5	1-3-6
6	1-3-6-(3-7)
7	(1-2-5) – (1-3-6-(3-7))
8	1-4-8
9	1-4-8-(4-9)
10	(1-2-5)-(1-3-6-(3-7))-(1-4-8-(4-9))

Fig. 4.20: Order of interfaces tested using top-down integration of Fig. 4.19

If a set of modules and their interfaces can realize a functionality with minimal interaction with other modules, then a set of such modules and their interfaces is known as a sub-system. Each sub-system represents a functionality that can be independently implemented. In Fig 4.20, step 4,6,9 can be considered as sub-systems. A breadth-first search order is used in Fig 4.20. Similarly, depth-first-search order can also be used for the integration of modules.

In bottom-up integration, the integration starts with the modules at the lowest levels in the hierarchy and moves upwards till all modules are integrated.

Consider Figure 4.19. The order in which interfaces are tested in bottom-up integration is given in Fig 4.21.

Step	Interfaces to be tested
1	5-2
2	6-3, 7-3
3	6-3-(7-3)
4	8-4, 9-4
5	8-4-(9-4)
6	5-2-1
7	6-3-(7-3)-1
8	8-4-(9-4)-1
9	(5-2-1) – (6-3-(7-3)-1)-(8-4-(9-4)-1)

Fig. 4.21: Order of interfaces tested using bottom-up integration of Fig. 4.19

In sandwich or bi-directional integration, top-down and bottom-up integration approaches are used together. To realize the bi-directional integration testing, stubs and drivers are used. This is required as the module which has to be integrated might not be developed or is under development. Stubs provide downstream connectivity of modules, whereas the drivers provide upstream connectivity. *Stubs* are functions that are used to simulate the functionality of the modules that are not yet integrated. They also simulate the behavior of missing modules, if any. Stubs are called programs used in top-down integration. *A driver* is a function that is used when the main module is not ready. Drivers are calling programs used in bottom-up integration. Consider a module hierarchy for a program as depicted in Fig. 4.22

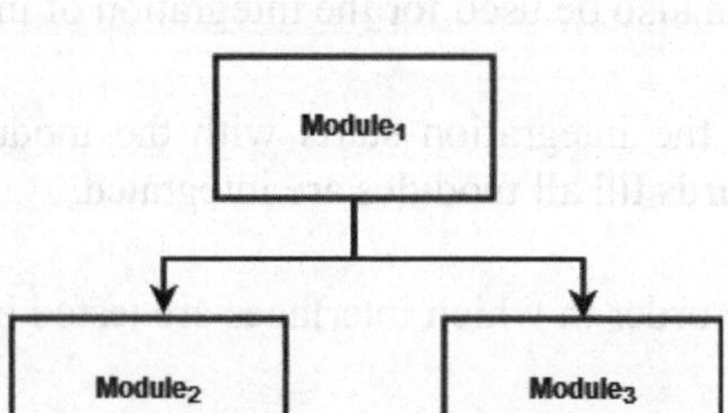

Fig. 4.22: Module hierarchy

There are three modules $Module_1$, $Module_2$, and $Module_3$. Assume that $Module_1$ is ready for the test, but other two modules, which $Module_1$ calls are not ready for testing. A piece of dummy code is written to simulate the functionality of $Module_2$ and $Module_3$. These dummy pieces of code are the stubs.

Consider a scenario (Fig 4.22), where $Module_2$ and $Module_3$ are ready, but $Module_1$ is not ready for testing. Since $Module_2$ and $Module_3$ return results to $Module_1$, a dummy code is written to simulate $Module_1$. This dummy piece of code is called the driver. Considering the Figure 4.19, the order in which interfaces are tested in sandwich integration is given in Fig 4.23.

Step	Interfaces to be tested
1	2-5
2	3-6-7
3	4-8-9
4	(1-2-5)-(1-3-6-7)-(1-4-8-9)

Fig. 4.23: Order of interfaces tested using sandwich integration of Fig. 4.19

Steps 1-3 in Fig 4.23 uses bottom-up integration, and step-4 uses a top-down integration mechanism.

In Big-bang integration, all system modules are integrated and tested as a single unit. Instead of integrating modules in several steps, the big-bang integration waits for all the modules to be ready for the test and performs integration. This strategy is used when most of the modules are already available and only some modules are added or modified. In such a case, instead of testing interfaces individually, all modules are integrated once and tested to save the resultant effort.

4.5.3 System Testing

System testing is performed on the complete integrated system to evaluate whether the functional and non-functional requirements are realized as per the expectation. System testing is product-level testing that helps identify defects that cannot be identified by testing a module or the integrated system. Test cases are written to test the overall functionality of the system. The non-functional or quality characteristics of the system, like performance, reliability, portability, interoperability, etc are tested. Stress testing helps in assessing the robustness of the software. This includes testing the system for abnormal conditions, checking the system's behavior after a failure, and asses the recovery process.

4.5.4 Acceptance Testing

The customer does acceptance testing. The customer tests the systems with real test cases to assess the system's quality. In agile methodologies, the acceptance test cases are written at the beginning jointly by the customer and sprint team. The acceptance test is executed to verify whether the end product meets the acceptance test criteria. Based on the outcome of the acceptance testing, the customer decides whether the product is accepted, rejected, or needs modification.

4.6 QUALITY ASSURANCE

Software quality refers to the system's compliance with the customer's expectations. Software is developed to satisfy the requirements given by the customer. Customer satisfaction depends on the proper transformation of requirements into a product such that the system's actual behavior meets the expected behavior. Quality control attempts to modify the product once the defects are detected. Quality control consists of defect detection and correction methods.

Quality assurance aims at defect prevention in the design and development process rather than defect detection and correction. Instead of testing a developed program, the quality assurance method will review the system's design before being converted to source code. Furthermore, the source code is ensured to meet the coding principles and practices.

4.6.1 Elements of Software Quality Assurance

Software quality assurance (SQA) includes activities that focus on managing the quality of a software system.

- **Standards**: Software engineering standards are provided by various organizations like ISO, IEC, IEEE, etc. The organizations may adopt these standards and ensure that the software developed complies with the adopted standards.

- **Reviews and Inspections**: Reviews, audits, and inspections are the quality control activities that can be carried out after completing each phase of software development. It ensures that the artifact produced is in accordance with set quality standards.

- **Testing**: Testing is done to find bugs. SQA ensures that the testing activities are properly planned and managed so that the testing goals are realized. SQA also analyzes the errors and faults produced so that appropriate processes are modified to address them in future

- **Change management**: Change is inevitable, but if it is not properly managed, it may lead to chaos and result in poor quality system. SQA ensures that a proper change management process is in place so that the quality of the software system is ensured.

- **Risk management**: Risk is a potential loss to the organization due to an unexpected event. SQA ensures that risks are analyzed and appropriately managed so the system does not result in costly failures.

- **Security management**: Each organization is expected to have policies to protect its systems and data. SQA needs to ensure that these policies are properly implemented and continuously give feedback to improve the policies.

UNIT SUMMARY

- ***Testing Preliminaries***
    - *Error, Fault, and Failure*
    - *Test Oracle*
    - *Verification and Validation*

- ***Testing Process***
    - *Requirements Analysis*
    - *Test Planning*
    - *Test Design*
    - *Environment Setup*
    - *Test Execution*
    - *Test Closure*

- ***Black Box Testing***
    - *Equivalence Class Partitioning*
    - *Boundary Value Analysis*
    - *Decision Table*
    - *Cause-Effect Graph*

- ***White Box Testing***
    - *Statement Coverage*
    - *Condition Coverage*
    - *Path Coverage*
    - *Function Coverage*

- ***Levels of Testing***
    - *Unit Testing*
    - *Integration Testing*
    - *System Testing*
    - *Acceptance Testing*

- ***Quality Assurance***
    - *Elements of Softwrare Quality Assurance*

EXERCISES

Multiple Choice Questions

4.1 The difference between the expected and actual outcome of a system is termed as

(a) Error (b) Fault (c) Failure (d) Detailed design

4.2 The mechanism that is used to determine whether the actual behavior confirms the expected behavior of the system is

(a) Fault (b) Test oracle (c) Test case (d) Test suite

4.3 The process in which the test cases are created before the development of the system with the help of the customer is

(a) Integration testing (b) System testing
(c) Test First Development (d) Acceptance testing

4.4 In onc of the following black box testing techniques, the input domain is divided into a finite number of groups

(a) Cause Effect Graphs (b) Decision trees
(c) Boundary value analysis (d) Equivalence class partitioning

4.5 The structural testing technique where all predicates are tested for each of the two possible outcomes is

(a) Statement coverage (b) Condition coverage
(c) Function coverage (d) Path coverage

4.6 The number of linearly independent paths in a program can be computed using

(a) Number of bugs (b) Number of faults
(c) Cyclomatic complexity (d) Number of failures

4.7 In one of the following methods, the integration of modules is both from the top and bottom of the hierarchy

(a) Top-down (b) Bottom-up
(c) Big-bang (d) Sandwich

4.8 The acceptance testing is performed by

(a) Customer (b) Programmer
(c) Tester (d) Developer

4.9 When the modules of the system are integrated and tested as a single unit, then it said to be

(a) Bottom-up integration (b) Big-bang integration
(c) Top-down integration (d) Sandwich integration

4.10 Quality control consists of

(a) Defect detection (b) Defect correction
(c) Defect prevention (d) Defect detection and correction

Answers of Multiple Choice Questions
4.1 (a), 4.2(b), 4.3(c), 4.4(d), 4.5(b), 4.6(c), 4.7(d), 4.8 (a), 4.9(b), 4.10 (d)

Short and Long Answer Type Questions

4.1 Differentiate between error, fault, and failure

4.2 What are the objectives of testing? Explain the testing process.

4.3 What is a test oracle? Why is it required

4.4 Differentiate between black box and white box testing

4.5 Compare and contrast (i) Verification and Validation (ii) Test case and Test suite

4.6 What are the guidelines for test case design?

4.7 What are stubs and drivers? Why are they needed

4.8 Explain levels of testing.

4.9 What is exhaustive testing? Why is it impractical

4.10 What is quality assurance? How is it different from quality control

PRACTICAL

4.1 Write a program to find the largest number from a given list of n- numbers. Draw the control flow graph and find the cyclomatic complexity. Design test cases to compute statement, condition and, path coverage.

4.2 Write a function to find the roots of a quadratic equation. Design test cases to perform black-box testing.

4.3 Design black box and white box test suite for the mini project you developed

KNOW MORE

Software testing is a tedious activity that requires a considerable amount of effort and time. Manual testing is not only time-consuming and costly but is error-prone. These issues can be addressed if the testing activity is automated. Testing tools help in reducing the effort of manual testing, and the testing can be done automatically.

There is no human involvement in automated testing so the testing activity can be done anytime. If the software has to be tested on different environments, testing tools help realize the same. This reduces the workforce and also reduces the error rate.

Testing the quality characteristics of a system may also be difficult manually. For example, performance testing can be carried out without many testers and hardware. The testing tools can simulate the behavior of multiple users on a single machine. The process of testing, including the test planning and test design, can also be adequately managed using testing tools. Test reports can also be generated automatically, which helps assess the software system's quality.

A wide range of software testing tools are available that are used to perform different types of testing. Functional testing tools are used to test application software and web applications. The application software generally involves several Graphical User Interfaces. The functional testing tools help test the GUI and associated functionality. These tools perform black box testing.

The source code testing tools test the application software's source code. These tools (AutomatedQAs, Aqtime, etc.) perform white box testing. Tools can compute the statement, condition, and path coverage. These tools also help check whether the source codes follow the standard coding guidelines and practices.

Performance testing tools (AutoTester's AutoController, Mercury, LoadRunner, Apache JMeter, etc.) are required for performance or stress testing. These tools help in simulating multiple users on a single machine. Java Testing Tools (Jemmy, Jmeter) are used to test Java applications.

Embedded testing tools (IBM Rational Test Real Time) test embedded software that includes complex tasks with stringent timing requirements to realize the applications. The Bug Tracking Tools (Samba's Jitterbug, GNU's GNATS, Segue Software's SkillRadar) are used by test engineers to report bugs and track bugs until they are removed.

REFERENCES AND SUGGESTED READINGS

- Sommerville, I. (2016). Software Engineering. 10th Edition, Pearson Education Limited, Boston
- Roger S. Pressman (2010). Software Engineering: A Practitioner's Approach, McGraw-Hill
- Rajib Mall (2018). Fundamentals of Software Engineering, 5th Edition, PHI Learning Private Limited.
- Pankaj Jalote (2010). Software Engineering: A Precise Approach, Wiley-India
- Srinivasan Desikan, Gopalaswamy Ramesh(2011). Software Testing Principles and Practices, Pearson-Education
- K.K. Aggarwal, Yogesh Singh(2008). Software Engineering, New Age International Publishers.
- IEEE Recommended Practice for Software Design Descriptions (1016-1998)

Dynamic QR Code for Further Reading

5 Project Management

UNIT SPECIFICS

Through this unit we have discussed the following aspects:

- *Project management Concepts;*
- *Configuration management;*
- *Release management;*
- *Version control;*
- *Change management;*
- *Software maintenance;*
- *Project metrics;*

The practical applications of the topics are discussed for generating further curiosity and creativity as well as improving problem solving capacity.

Besides giving multiple choice questions as well as questions of short and long answer types marked in two categories following lower and higher order of Bloom's taxonomy, assignments, a list of references and suggested readings are given in the unit so that one can go through them for practice. It is important to note that for getting more information on various topics of interest some QR codes have been provided in different sections which can be scanned for relevant supportive knowledge.

After the related practical, based on the content, there is a "Know More" section. This section has been carefully designed so that the supplementary information provided in this part becomes beneficial for the users of the book. This section mainly highlights the initial activity, examples of some interesting facts, analogy, history of the development of the subject focusing the salient observations and finding, timelines starting from the development of the concerned topics up to the recent time, applications of the subject matter for our day-to-day real life or/and industrial applications on variety of aspects, case study related to environmental, sustainability, social and ethical issues whichever applicable, and finally inquisitiveness and curiosity topics of the unit.

RATIONALE

Software development is a time-bound activity, where the software is expected to be delivered within time, given budget, and satisfying the desired quality characteristics. The software development activity must be properly planned, managed, and controlled to develop a quality product within time and budget. Project management is a discipline that helps manage the project's progress to achieve the desired specific, measurable, achievable, realistic, and time-bound outcome. In order to realize these goals, a project manager is expected to plan, control, and monitor each software development activity.

According to a recent survey by Project Management Institute, 45% of projects miss delivery dates, 38% of projects miss budget targets, 27% fail to meet organizational goals, and 34% of projects' scope gets changed. The responsibility of a project manager includes planning, organizing, budgeting, managing tasks, and controlling costs using tools and techniques.

A software project often goes through changes during development and after the delivery of the software to the customer. Hence, there is a need to manage the changes systematically. The various artifacts produced during software development, like requirements specification, software design document, source code, and user manual etc., are developed and modified by various people involved in the project development. Software Configuration Management (SPM) tracks and manages the state of these artifacts.

The customer may request changes in software during the development or after the deployment of the software. The systematic approach to modify the software after its delivery is software maintenance. These changes have to be managed and tracked. Change management is the systematic approach to managing, controlling, and adapting changes. There may be various versions of the artifacts during the development and even after software delivery. Version control is the systematic approach to tracking and managing various versions of artifacts of the given software system.

This unit helps students to understand software project management activities. This includes software planning, configuration management, version control, change management, maintenance, and metrics.

PRE-REQUISITES

Computer Programming (Diploma Semester-III)

Scripting Languages (Diploma Semester-III)

UNIT OUTCOMES

List of outcomes of this unit is as follows:

U5-O1: Understand the project planning activities.

U5-O2: Apply techniques for effort estimation and scheduling

U5-O3: Understand software configuration management

U5-O4: Understand software maintenance and change management activities

U5-O5: Understand the software metrics.

Unit-5 Outcomes	EXPECTED MAPPING WITH COURSE OUTCOMES (1- Weak Correlation; 2- Medium correlation; 3- Strong Correlation)				
	CO-1	CO-2	CO-3	CO-4	CO-5
U5-O1	2	2	1	1	3
U5-O2	2	2	1	1	3
U5-O3	2	2	1	1	3
U5-O4	2	2	1	1	3
U5-05	2	2	1	1	3

5.1 Project Management Concepts

Software development aims to produce quality products within the allocated time and budget. As there could be various issues during the development process, it is indispensable that each activity of the development has to be managed, tracked, and controlled. Project managers add value to the organization by interacting and communicating with all stakeholders to ensure that the end product is high quality. Software project management is a systematic approach to ensuring quality in software development in terms of cost, schedule, and customer satisfaction. Many software projects are not realized successfully, and those completed are out of planned timelines, incurring higher costs than planned and to customers' dissatisfaction. The lack of software quality is due to inadequate project management.

According to the various scientific studies (KPMG 1995; The Standish Group 1995; Jones 1996; Putnam and Myers 1997; Pressman 1997; Royce 1998), there are three main reasons for the failure of software projects. This includes inadequate project planning, project management, and methods unsuited for software projects.

5.1.1 The Management Spectrum

The four essential components of project management are People, Product, Process, and Project.

- **People**: A successful team's involvement makes any project's success possible. The team's collective effort will lead to delivering a quality product within defined time limits and an assigned budget. Various stakeholders are required for the successful realization of projects. This includes the customer, project leader, project manager, and software team. The software team comprises analysts, architects, designers, programmers, and testers. The project manager needs to coordinate and communicate with all stakeholders, from initiating to delivering the product.

- **Product:** The final artifact of the software development is a product. The product objectives and scope need to be defined before planning the project. The stakeholders interact in finalizing the objectives and scope. Objectives indicate the goals of the product as per the customer's need. The scope identifies the desired characteristics, functions, and behaviour that are desired from the product. Once the objectives and scope are adequately understood, complete, and unambiguous, several alternative solutions are required to implement the desired functionality. The complexity of the desired functionality can be reduced by partitioning the system into several manageable units. These alternative solutions help the project managers to select an appropriate solution based on the given constraints. The constraints could concern delivery time, budget, resource, and human resources availability etc.

- **Process:** A Software process defines the set of activities that helps in developing software. These activities mainly apply to all software projects, irrespective of their complexity and size. However, the appropriate team selects a particular process model to develop the software by considering the given constraints. Once the process model is selected, a preliminary project plan is established, which will be refined further. Each functionality of the project is listed. These activities help the project manager estimate the schedule, cost, and resources required to realize the same.

- **Project:** According to a recent survey by Project Management Institute, about 27% of projects were successful, were realized within the planned schedule and cost, and achieved the desired quality objectives. 45% of projects experience time overruns, and about 38% experience cost overruns. To manage a project, knowing which problems can be avoided is imperative.

There are several reasons for failing to achieve the desired software quality within a specified time and budget. This includes the following:

- Incomplete, ambiguous, and inconsistent requirements.
- Unrealistic deadlines
- Incorrect scope defined
- Lack of people with appropriate skills
- Poor change management

A project manager is responsible for guiding the team and ensuring that the project's progress is within the defined scope and meets the given deadlines. A project manager is expected to communicate with the team and make appropriate decisions for the successful realization of the software. The functionalities of a project manager can be broadly classified into two categories: (i) Planning (ii) Monitoring and Control.

5.1.2 W^5HH principle

Boehm [1996] suggested a mechanism that helps identify proper objectives, deciding schedules, resources, and milestones. The W^5HH principle is used to identify the critical project characteristics and thereby helps in realizing a project plan.

- *Why is the system being developed*?
  The need for development of the software needs to be assessed by the stakeholders. Furthermore, the feasibility of developing the system economically, technically and operationally has to be assessed.
- *What will be done?*
  The features of the desired system have to be listed, and the specific tasks are defined. This helps in defining the scope of the project.
- *When will it be done?*
  The project schedule is established by estimating the schedule of each of the tasks of the system.
- *Who will be responsible*?
  The responsibilities of each member of the software team are defined. The project manager assigns responsibilities based on the project and teams strengths.
- *Where are they located?*
  Not all stakeholders may reside in one place. Furthermore, the software team may also be geographically distributed.

- *How much of resources is needed?*
  Based on the scope and features identified, one has to estimate the human resources and other resources required for development of the system.

- *How will job be done technically and managerially?*
  A management and technical strategy for developing the project is defined as the product scope is established.

5.2 PROJECT SIZE ESTIMATION METRICS

Planning is the primary step in project management activity. If there is no proper plan, it isn't easy to monitor or control the project's progress. Lack of adequate planning may fail the project as no effort, schedule, or resource estimates are available. Planning aims to identify the activities required to implement the project successfully. Scheduling of activities and identification of resources to realize each activity is to be identified by considering the given constraints.

Once the feasibility of a system is assessed, project objectives and scope are clearly defined, and the project planning is undertaken before starting the development process. The primary activities of project planning and management are:

- Estimation: This includes an assessment of the cost and effort required for the development of software and the time taken to develop the software.
- Scheduling: It specifies project tasks, their durations, and dependencies.
- Staffing: The organization of a team and selection of the proper set of people for the given tasks need to be identified based on the need.
- Risk Management: Risk engineering that includes risk identification, analysis, and risk aversion strategies must be planned.
- Configuration management, release, and change management activities should be planned.

Size is the fundamental input based on which other estimates are dependent. Size is an input to compute the effort required to develop the project and the duration of development. The cost of the project is computed as a function of effort estimation. The estimated cost helps in negotiations of the actual price with the customers. Staffing and scheduling of activities are possible once the assessments are made.

As planning is a critical activity, wrong estimates may lead to delays in the delivery of projects, and the project may also fail. Project managers often refine the plan regularly because the clarity increases as the project progresses.

Precise project size estimation helps accurately estimate the effort, time duration, and project cost. Lines of Code and Function points are the two fundamental techniques to estimate the project size. Each method has its advantages and disadvantages.

5.2.1 Lines of Code (LOC)

LOC is a metric that measures the size of the project by counting the number of lines of code in the program. The comments and headers, if any, are ignored while calculating the number of lines. The number of lines of code is also known as Delivered Source code Instructions (DSI) or Source Lines of Code (SLOC).

LOC can be easily determined at the end of the project. However, LOCs have to be estimated before the start of the development to estimate effort, time, and cost. Generally, LOC is estimated based on experience and a calculated guess. Project managers also count the number of lines of code by decomposing the problem into various modules. Each module can be further decomposed until the number of lines of code at the lower level can be estimated. By using the estimate of all leaf levels, the project's total size is estimated.

LOC measure has several disadvantages. There can be different ways to write code for the same logic. For the same problem, the number of lines of code may vary. An instruction can also be written in multiple lines, which can be addressed by counting language tokens. Secondly, LOC only considers the source lines of code but doesn't consider the effort required for analysis, design, testing, etc. The design may require extra effort due to the problem's complexity, but the number of source lines is fewer or vice versa. In such cases, size estimation may not precisely represent the actual effort. Thirdly, the LOC measure only counts the number of lines of source code and doesn't consider the code quality. The programs may be lengthy sometimes, but the code must meet the quality requirements.
Further, the number of lines of code will be fewer when high-level programming languages are used for coding. The number of lines of code for the same logic may also differ from one programming language to the other. Therefore, the LOC metric is not a feasible measure to estimate the size of the project as the effort, cost, and time estimates have to be done before the development begins.

5.2.2 Function Point (FP)

Function Point metric proposed by Albrecht [1983] addresses the drawbacks of the LOC measure. In contrast to the LOC measure, the function point technique estimates the project size from the requirements specification. In function point metric, the size of a project is estimated based on the number of features of the given system. The size of the system depends on various factors. A system is composed of several functions. Each function takes inputs and produces output. A system's inputs and output values help determine the number of functionalities. Furthermore, the size depends on the number of files and interfaces required to store and retrieve the data to realize a function.

The function point approach uses five parameters: external inputs, external outputs, internal files, interfaces, and inquiries. These parameters capture the functionality of the system. Two elements of the same type may have different levels of complexity. The complexity of each parameter can be classified as Simple, Average, or Complex.

The unique input to the application from external sources like input screens, external databases, external files, etc., is counted as external inputs. Similarly, each output that leaves the system boundary is counted as an external output. External output can be messages, files, or log reports. The number of user inquiries that require a specific response from the system is counted. Each application maintains information to perform functionality. A function may read data from a data store, process it, and update the output back in the data store. This file, which maintains records, is counted as an internal file. The external files are the files that are shared between applications.

The function point is calculated using the following steps.

Step 1: Compute the count of all five parameters, namely external inputs, external outputs, inquiries, internal files, and external files.

Step 2: Assign the complexity of each element in a given parameter. (Two elements of the same type may have different complexity). Function point parameters and their complexities are specified in Figure 5.1

Type	Simple	Average	Complex
External Inputs (EI)	3	4	6
External Outputs (EO)	4	5	7
Inquiries (I)	3	4	6
Internal Files (IF)	7	10	15
External Files (EF)	5	7	10

Fig. 5.1: FP Analysis parameters and weighing factors

Step 3: Compute the Unadjusted Function Point (UFP) as a weighted sum

$$UFP = \sum_{\substack{1 \le i \le 5 \\ 1 \le j \le 3}} \text{Wij.Cij}$$

Wij represents the weight of an element of type i and complexity j
Cij represents the count of the number of elements of type i classified as having weight corresponding to column j.

Step 4: Compute Complexity Adjustment Factor (CAF). UFP is adjusted with 14 characteristics that influence the development effort. The 14 characteristics are data communications, distributed processing, performance objectives, operation configuration load, transaction rate, online data entry, end-user efficiency, online update, complex processing logic, reusability, installation ease, operational ease, multiple sites, and facilitate change. Each factor is assigned a value from 0 (not present or no influence) to 5 (strong influence).

$$CAF = 0.65 + 0.01 * \sum_{i=1}^{14} fi$$

CAF ranges from 0.65 to 1.35.

Step 5: Compute Function point

FP = UFP * CAF (FP can differ from UFP at most by 35 %)

There is a correlation between the function points and the size of the software. This depends on the programming language used. According to several studies in literature, one function point is estimated as 125 lines of code in C language and 50 lines of code in Java or C++.

Example: For a given application, let the count of five parameters be EI=20 (simple), EO=12 (Average), I = 7 (Complex), IF=5 (Average), EF=4 (Complex).

Then UFP = (20 * 3) + (12 * 5) + (7 * 6) + (5 * 10) + (4 * 10) = 252

Assume that all 14 parameters have average influence (3) in the given project, then CAF = 0.65 + 0.01 (14*3) = 1.07.

In the given example, FP = 252 * 1.07 = 269.64 (In this case, the UFP is adjusted by 7%)

Assuming that the application is to be developed in C language, each function point is expected to take 125 LOC, then the size of the project = 269.64 * 125 = 33705 LOC=33.705 KLOC.

The function point approach is computed subject to complete, consistent, and unambiguous requirements. The function point metric does not consider the complexity of the algorithm. It assumes that the effort required to design, develop, and test functionalities is the same. To overcome this problem, the feature point metric, an extension to function point, is proposed. The function point metric additionally considers algorithm complexity.

5.3 SOFTWARE PLANNING

Once the size of the project is estimated, it is desirable to estimate the cost of the software and the time taken for the development. These estimates are required before the development begins. The project manager will use the cost and schedule estimates to realize monitoring and control activities. The major part of the software development cost is the staffing requirement. Most estimation techniques estimate effort as a unit of person-months (PM). The other costs, including the cost of software, hardware, and other resources, are included to estimate the project's total cost. These estimates also help in resource planning and scheduling.

5.3.1 Effort Estimation: COCOMO

The effort can be estimated in the bottom-up estimation technique if the size of the project is calculated accurately. The steps to be followed in the bottom-up estimation approach are as follows:

- Determine modules of the system and estimate the size of each module
- Determine the initial effort of each module (as a function of LOC)
- Determine the effort multipliers of each module
- Adjust the effort by multiplying the initial estimate with the effort adjustment factor (product of effort multipliers)
- Estimate the time for development, which is a function of effort.
- Estimate the cost of the project.

Constructive Cost Model (COCOMO) was proposed by Boehm (1981). As the effort varies from one type of project to another, software development projects can be divided into three categories. This includes Organic, Semi-detached, and Embedded. The three categories correspond to application, utility, and system projects, respectively. Additionally, organic-type projects are generally applications with a clear understanding of requirements, smaller projects, and involving an experienced team that develops projects in a similar domain. In semi-detached mode, the team involved experienced and inexperienced staff. In embedded-type projects, there is a strong correlation between the software being developed and the hardware. According to Boehm, the cost estimation is done in three stages: Basic COCOMO, Intermediate COCOMO, and Advanced COCOMO.

In *Basic COCOMO*, the effort is computed as a function of the number of thousand lines of code (KLOC). The following expressions estimate Effort and Time for Development (Tdev).

$$Effort = a * (KLOC)^b \, PM$$
$$Tdev = c * (Effort)^d \, Months$$

Where KLOC is the size of the software product expressed in Kilo Lines of Code
a, b, c, d are constants of each category of the software project (Figure 5.2)
Effort is the effort required to develop the software, expressed in person-months (PM)
T_{dev} is the estimated time for the development of software, expressed in months

System	a	b	c	d
Organic	2.4	1.05	2.5	0.38
Semi-detached	3.0	1.12	2.5	0.35
Embedded	3.6	1.20	2.5	0.32

Fig. 5.2: Constant values for various systems to compute effort and Time

Example: The size of a given organic mode system is 35000 lines of code. Let the average salary of the developer be Rs. 30,000/= per month. Determine effort required to develop the software, time for development, and development cost. Assume that total overhead constitutes Rs. 1, 00,000/=

As the project is of organic type, the constant values are a=2.4, b=1.05, c=2.5, d=0.38
Effort = $2.4 * (35)^{1.05}$ = 100.34 PM
Tdev = $2.5 * (100.34)^{0.38}$ = 14.4 months.

Cost of the project = (Effort * Salary of developer) + overhead cost
= (100.34 * 30000) + 100000
= Rs. 31, 10, 200/=

Number of Developers = Effort/Tdev = 100.34/14.4 = 6.96 $\approx$7 persons

In basic COCOMO, the effort and time for development are functions of the number of lines of code only. However, the effort depends on various other factors. If the complexity is high, then the effort needs to be more. Similarly, if the developers are experienced, then their salary might be high, and so on. The *Intermediate COCOMO* model considers the effort multipliers to adjust the initial effort computed using the number of lines of code. These effort multipliers are classified into four broader groups: Product, Computer, Personnel, and Project attributes. A total of 15 attributes (effort multipliers) are assigned values based on their complexities (Fig. 5.3). The Effort Adjustment Factor (EAF) is the product of all effort multipliers (Ei)

$$EAF = \prod_{i=1}^{i=15} E_i$$

Cost Drivers	Rating				
	Very Low	Low	Nominal	High	Very High
Product Attributes					
Required Reliability	0.75	0.88	1.00	1.15	1.40
Database Size	--	0.94	1.00	1.08	1.16
Product Complexity	0.70	0.85	1.00	1.15	1.30
Computer Attributes					
Execution Time	--	--	1.00	1.11	1.30
Storage constraint	--	--	1.00	1.06	1.21
Virtual machine volatility	--	0.87	1.00	1.15	1.30
Turnaround time	--	0.87	1.00	1.07	1.15
Personal Attributes					
Analyst capability	1.46	1.19	1.00	0.86	0.71
Application experience	1.29	1.13	1.00	0.91	0.82
Programmer capability	1.42	1.17	1.00	0.86	0.70
Virtual machine experience	1.21	1.10	1.00	0.90	--
Prog language experience	1.14	1.07	1.00	0.95	--
Project Attributes					
Modern progr. Practices	1.24	1.10	1.00	0.91	0.82
Use of Software tools	1.24	1.10	1.00	0.91	0.83
Development schedule	1.23	1.08	1.00	1.04	1.10

Fig. 5.3: Effort multipliers for different cost drivers

The resultant effort is computed as a product of the initial effort estimate and the Effort Adjustment Factor (EAF)

$$\text{Effort (E)} = E_{\text{initial}} * EAF$$

Example: The size of a given embedded mode project is 38000 lines of code. Let the average salary of the developer be Rs. 30,000/= per month. Determine the effort required to develop the software, time for development. Consider the cost drivers: RELY=0.88, DATA=1.08, CPLX= 1.30, TIME=1.30, STOR=1.21, and all other cost drivers as nominal (Effort multiplier=1).

As the project is of organic type, the constant values are a=3.6, b=1.20, c=2.5, d=0.32

$\text{Effort}_{\text{initial}} = 3.6 * (38)^{1.20} = 78.66$ PM

EAF = 0.88 * 1.08 * 1.30 * 1.30 * 1.21 * 1 = 1.94

$\text{Effort} = \text{Effort}_{\text{initial}} * \text{EAF} = 78.66 * 1.94 = 152.6$ PM

$\text{Tdev} = 2.5 * (152.6)^{0.32} = 12.5$ months.

Number of Developers = Effort/Tdev = 152.6/12.5 = 12.2 ≈12 persons

The drawback of the intermediate COCOMO model is that it considers the software as a single entity. The effort multipliers are the same for the entire project. Practically, the complexity of each module or activity may vary. Further, many large systems are composed of sub-systems, and each sub-system's complexity may differ. The *Advanced COCOMO* model is similar to intermediate COCOMO. However, it estimates the size of each module or activity. The effort multipliers for each activity or module are assessed to compute the effort and time for the development of each module. The sum of the efforts of each module is computed to estimate the effort for the development of the system. Similarly, the total time for development is estimated.

5.3.2 Project Scheduling and Staffing

Once the effort is estimated, the schedule, which indicates the project's duration, is estimated. The resources (human resources) required to develop the project are also estimated. In the COCOMO model, once effort and time for development are computed, the number of people required to develop the project can be evaluated. If a project effort is 72 person-months and the total schedule is nine months, then eight people are required for development. A schedule of eight months with nine people is also possible. However, the manpower and time duration are not entirely interchangeable. For example, it may not be possible to complete the project in one month by employing 72 people.

The total duration of the project, estimated using the effort and time for development parameters, may not help the project managers manage and control various project activities. This is because the schedule of various project activities is not estimated. However, the overall schedule helps in deciding the project's delivery time.

Work Breakdown Structure (WBS) divides the system into activities. The project manager may decide on these activities based on the manpower available and their core strengths in realizing these activities. A general format of work-break down structure is given in Figure 5.4

Task Name	Duration	Predecessor task	Expected		Manpower	Other Resources	Actual	
			Start Date	End Date			Start Date	End Date

Fig. 5.4: Work Breakdown Structure

The task name specifies the activities and tasks identified by the project manager. The duration of completion of each task is estimated. The predecessor task is the task which has to be completed before the current task begins. This helps to know the dependencies between the tasks. The project manager estimates the expected start date and end dates base don the duration. It can be in weeks, hours, or minutes as well. The manpower or the personnel responsible for executing the task is also identified. Any other resource requirements to execute that task are also identified. In order to manage and control the activities, the project manager needs to look at the actual start and end date. In case of a delay, the project manager is expected to communicate with the team to see that there are no further delays. Sometimes, the slack (extra time) available because of dependency will help in manage the delays.

A project manager is expected to follow the following activities for scheduling the project tasks

- Identify tasks required in the project
- Divide the tasks into activities
- Identify the dependency, if any, between different tasks
- Estimate the time duration to complete each task
- Allocate resources to each task/activity
- Plan the expected start date and end date of each activity
- Determine the critical path.

Consider a sample WBS given in Figure 5.5

Task Name	**Duration (days)**	**Predecessor**	**Expected**		**Resources**
			Start Date	**End Date**	
T_1	10	-	1st Sept	10th Sept	
T_2	6	T_1	11th Sept	16th Sept	
T_3	3	T_2	17th Sept	19th Sept	
T_4	11	T_3	20th Sept	30th Sept	
T_5	7	T_3	20th Sept	26th Sept	
T_6	4	T_4 , T_5	1st Oct	4th Oct	
T_7	6	T_6	5th Oct	10th Oct	

Fig. 5.5: Work Breakdown Structure example

WBS representation can be represented as an activity network that represents activities identified in WBS as nodes and their dependencies as the edges. The activity network representation of Figure 5.5 is given in Figure 5.6

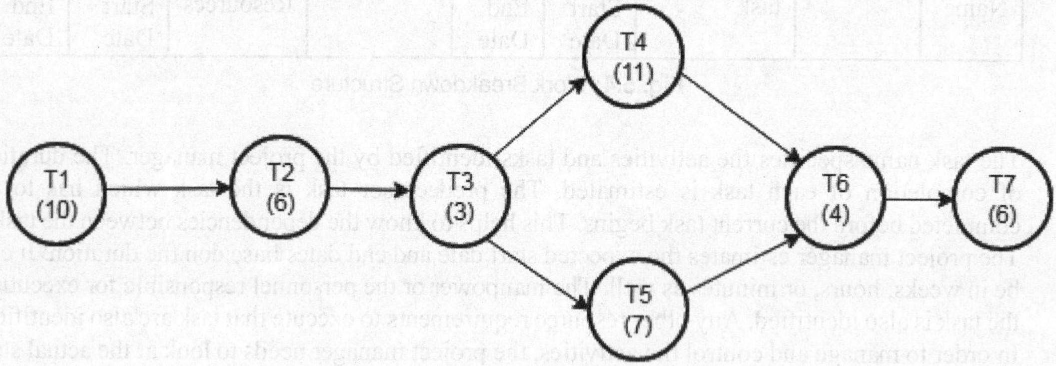

Fig. 5.6: Activity network representation of Fig. 5.5

The following analysis can be made on the activity network representation

- The minimum time (MT) required to complete the project is the maximum of all paths from beginning to end.
  MT = 10 + 6 + 3 + 11 + 4 + 6 =40 days
- The Earliest start time(EST) of a task Ti is the maximum of all paths from the starting node to Ti.
- Early Finish time (EFT) is the sum of the earliest start time and duration of the task.
- The Latest Start time (LST) is the difference between the minimum time (MT) and maximum of all paths from the current task to the end.
- The Latest Finish time (LFT) of a task can be obtained by subtracting the maximum of all paths from this task to finish from MT.
- Slack Time (ST) is the time that delays a task without delaying the project. ST = LFT-EFT

Task Name	EST	EFT	LST	LFT	ST
T_1	0	10	0	10	0
T_2	10	16	10	16	0
T_3	16	19	16	19	0
T_4	19	30	19	30	0
T_5	19	26	23	30	4
T_6	30	34	30	34	0
T_7	34	40	34	40	0

Fig. 5.7: Critical path analysis of Fig. 5.6

Critical paths are the paths whose duration is equal to the minimum time (MT). The Critical path of Fig 5.6 is T_1-T_2-T_3-T_4-T_6-T_7.

Gantt charts are used in resource planning. Each activity has to be associated with resources. Gantt chart is a type of bar chart where the bar represents an activity shown along a time line. Project managers use Gantt chart for resource monitoring and control. Gantt chart representation of Fig 5.5 is shown in Fig. 5.8.

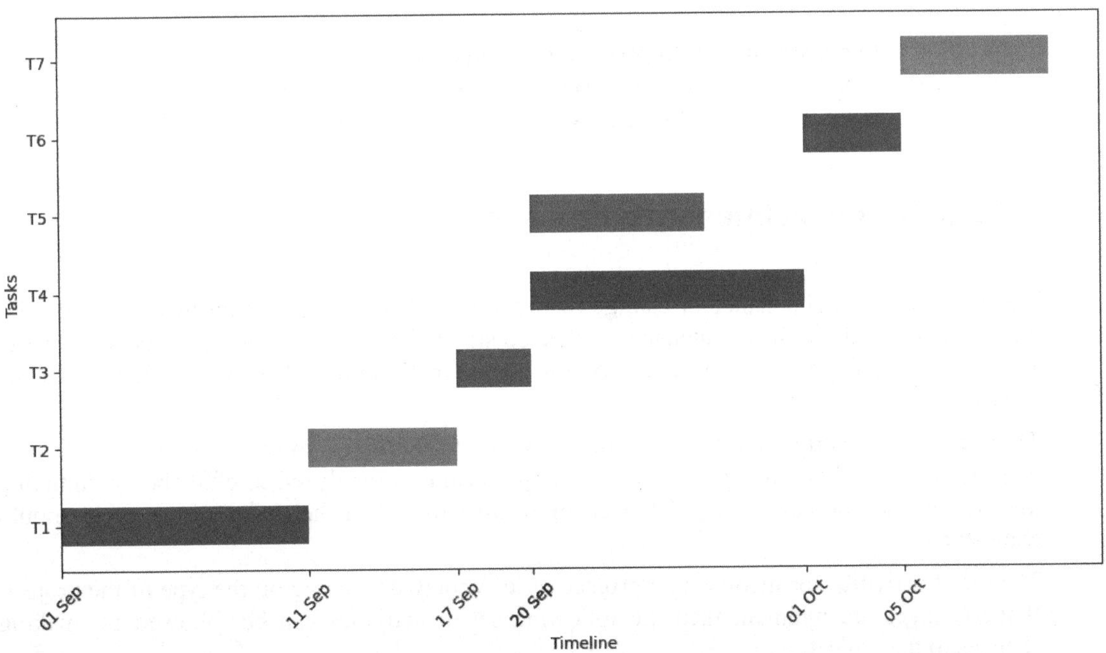

Fig. 5.8: Gantt chart representation of Fig. 5.5

5.4 SOFTWARE MAINTENANCE

Modifications made to software product after its delivery to the customer is referred to as software maintenance. Maintenance is generally needed when certain failures are reported while using the system, specific changes are required in existing requirements, or a new functionality must be incorporated. The effort required to modify a system also needs to be computed. Whenever software is adapted to new environments, changes are needed.

5.4.1 Types of Software Maintenance

Software maintenance is broadly classified into three categories:

- Corrective maintenance: The changes to the software are requested to fix the bugs that are identified while using the system. Generally such requests are about 20% of the total maintenance requests.
- Adaptive maintenance: The changes to the software are needed when the customer wants to run the software on new platforms on new operating systems or when it requires interfacing with other devices. Such requests are about 25%
- Perfective maintenance: In perfective maintenance, customers request changes in system functionalities, and the changes are also requested when new functionalities or features are to be added to the existing system. Such requests are about 55%.

5.4.2 Software Maintenance Process

The activities for maintenance or change requests depend on several parameters. This includes the resources required for maintenance, expected side effects due to changes to the system etc. Adaptive or perfective maintenance requires a systematic approach to make changes to the software.

There could be multiple requests for modifications to the given software. There is a need to manage and track these changes. The change requests must be analyzed carefully before initiating the maintenance process. Only if the changes are valid, then the maintenance cycle should commence.

The set of activities for modifying a project varies widely depending on the type of the project. If the changes are minimal, then the following set of activities can be followed for making changes to the project.

- Get change request: In this step, the change requirements are collected.
- Analyze the change request: The changes are analyzed, and the feasibility of the requested modification is assessed.
- Decision on change request acceptance: A modification request id (MR_i) is assigned if the change request is accepted. This is used to manage and track the changes.
- Plan Change: The effort, time, cost required for maintenance is estimated.
- Design and implementation: The requested changes are designed and implemented
- Integration: The tested modifications are integrated with the existing system
- Regression testing: The testing that is performed after making changes to the system is regression testing. It has to be ensured that new modifications are implemented and, at the same time, existing modifications should not be affected.
- Update documents: The software assets, such as SRS, Design documents, and test reports, must be updated with the changes. Once maintenance activity is completed, the maintenance request is closed.

The above activities are possible if the same team has taken the modification request that has developed the system. However, if the team that has taken the change request is a different team, then there is a need to get insight into the existing system before the change request is initiated. This is possible through reverse engineering, where the source code is translated to design to understand the existing system. Then, the change request is considered, and the above-stated steps are followed to make changes to the system.

5.4.3 Maintenance cost estimation

The maintenance cost varies from one project to another. According to Boehm (1981) the maintenance cost estimation depends on the Annual Change Traffic (ACT) parameter.

$$ACT = \frac{KLOC_{added} + KLOC_{deleted}}{KLOC_{total}}$$

Where KLOC added is the KLOC added during the change process

KLOC deleted is the total KLOC deleted during the change process

The maintenance cost is estimated by multiplying the annual change traffic (ACT) with the development cost.

$$Maintenance\ cost = ACT * Development\ cost$$

The maintenance estimation technique only gives an approximate cost, as the cost drivers and other resource costs are not considered in estimating maintenance costs.

5.5 SOFTWARE CONFIGURATION MANAGEMENT

Changes to software systems are common as most of the development work is on maintenance. The software development artifacts consist of SRS, software plan, software design document, source code, test suites, user manuals etc. Whenever some changes are incorporated, the state of these documents changes. The state of all the artifacts of the software system at any point in time is referred to as configuration of the software product.

Software Configuration Management (SCM) or change management represents a set of activities to track, control, and manage changes by identifying the artifacts that are likely to change, specifying mechanisms to manage different versions of the system, and auditing and reporting on the changes done. A hierarchy of software configuration items (SCI) is created as software is being developed. SCI can be as small as a use case diagram or as large as a software design document. Changes to SCI may happen at any time.

Change to a software system may happen because of the following reasons

- Budget, resource, or schedule constraints require change in the scope of the system
- Business or market economic conditions may need changes to the system
- The users of the system may request modifications to the system.
- Changes may also happen because of a feature being introduced by a competitor.

5.5.1 Software Configuration Management Process

The Software Configuration Management (SCM) tools help the project manager to track various artifacts. This will help the Project Manager identify any artifact's current state. The configuration management tools help the developer to perform changes to the system in a controlled manner. Examples of configuration management tools include GIT, Ansible, CFEngine etc. SCM process specifies a series of tasks for different artifacts of software. This includes

- Configuration identification
- Change Control
- Version Control
- Auditing
- Reporting

In the ***configuration identification*** phase, the software configuration items are identified. During this process, two types of objects are identified. A basic object is an SCI that is created during requirements engineering, analysis, design, implementation, or test. An object can be a part of requirements specification or a part of design, function of a module, or a test case. The collection of basic objects forms an aggregate object. In the configuration identification phase, aggregate objects include the Architectural model, Data model, Component etc. Each object identified has features that include its name, description, characteristics, and resources. Object resources include functions, data types etc. The configuration identification phase also considers the relationships that exist between objects. The changes to these objects require monitoring and control to ensure that changes to a system happen without any side effects.

Changes to SCIs need to be managed and controlled. Several change requests are received, but it has to be analyzed whether the changes are desired. The ***change control*** process is depicted in Figure 5.9

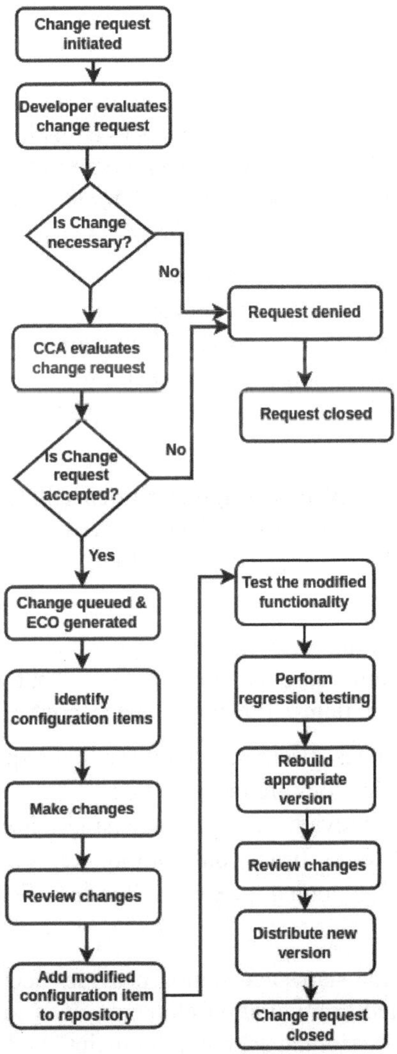

Fig. 5.9: Software Configuration Management Process

The stakeholder submits a change request. The developer evaluates the modification requested to assess the foreseen side effects because its impact on configuration objects and estimates the effort for performing the changes. If it is feasible to proceed with the changes, the request is submitted to the change control authority (CCA), which decides whether to proceed with the changes. An ECO (Engineering Change Order) or Modification Request id (MRi) is generated for each such request. The changes are made and reviewed. The affected configuration items due to the change are added to the repository with appropriate versioning. Testing for the desired changes is done, followed by regression testing, which needs to ensure that the side effects due to the change do not exist or are minimized. The version of the product is decided and the CCA reviews the final artifact. After approval of CCA, the new version is distributed and the request is closed.

Version Control: As the various activities of software are being developed, several versions of configuration items are created. A repository is to be maintained that keeps track of all versions of configuration items. This will permit developers to review earlier releases during testing. A version control specifies the procedures and tools that can manage different versions of configuration items. The following are the characteristics of a version control system.

- Maintains a project database that stores software configuration items
- Changes to each configuration item are maintained as different versions in the database.
- Make facility that helps the development team use existing relevant configuration items and develop a functionality that can be reused.
- The bug tracing feature enables us to document issues with each configuration item.

If the characteristics of a software configuration item (SCI) are maintained in the database along with reasons for change, then it helps in the effective reuse of existing artifacts. This is achieved by using a software configuration management tool.

Configuration audit is required to ensure that the requested changes are properly realized. A software configuration audit assesses characteristics that are not considered during technical review of the configuration items. The audit expects conformance to following parameters

- Whether the changes specified in modification request are implemented
- Any other modifications are incorporated
- Whether technical review of suggested changes is conducted
- Whether the related software configuration items are updated.
- Whether proper versioning for each SCI is specified and is updated in the repository.

Reporting or Configuration status accounting provides accurate information about the software product and its associated configuration elements. It is to ensure that the historical status of configuration items and versioning are correctly maintained and can be traced. It also keeps track of what changes have been done by whom, when, and where.

5.5.2 Release Management

Release management is a process of planning, scheduling, monitoring, and controlling software releases. It must ensure that different software releases are delivered to the customer per the release plan.

Release management starts with a request to develop new software or to make changes to the existing system. Every request cannot be translated to a new release, so its feasibility is evaluated. After ensuring that the system is feasible to develop, the most essential activity is to plan the release.

In release planning, the builds or deliverables are planned. This depends on the type of development methodology adopted. In incremental and rapid application development approaches, several software releases exist. In agile methods, the Product backlog specifies various stories and their tasks. Once the sprint is developed and tested, it is ready for release. Each task of the sprint is planned. The time taken for each task, resources required, and the priority are planned. The release management process must ensure that the sprints are released per the sprint plan. Several versions of releases need to be maintained and monitored. The advantage of release management is that as the builds are maintained, any new system must not start from scratch. The existing releases can be modified to deliver the quality product within time and budget. A release is successful if deployed within the estimated time and budget and satisfies the customer's needs.

A generic release plan for a system that is released using agile methodology is specified in Figure 5.10

Task Name	Priority	Time (in days)	Resources
Sprint 1	High	5	
Task 1	Medium	2	
Task 2	Medium	2	
Task 3	Medium	1	
Sprint 2	Medium	13	
Task 4	Medium	4	
Task 5	Low	6	
Task 6	Medium	3	

Fig. 5.10: Sample Product Backlog

In Fig 5.10, there are two sprints. Sprint-1 is of high priority and is expected to be released first. For each task, the priority and time are estimated. The total estimated time for story 1 is five days. The story-1 is expected to be released in 5 days. If sprint-2 depends on sprint-1, it will be released in the next 13 days. However, multiple teams can also work on several sprints. In such a case, the release plan needs to be modified. Some agile approaches, like extreme programming (XP), use a test-first development (TFD) approach. The release management process needs to ensure that the acceptance test cases planned for each task in the release are successful before testing the entire sprint.

UNIT SUMMARY

- ***Project Management Concepts***
    - *The Management Spectrum*
    - *W^5HH Principle*

- ***Project Size Estimation Metrics***
    - *Lines of Code (LOC)*
    - *Function Point Model*

- ***Software Planning***
    - *Effort Estimation: COCOMO*
    - *Project Scheduling & Staffing*

- ***Software Maintenance***
    - *Types of Software Maintenance*
    - *Maintenance process*
    - *Maintenance cost estimation*

- ***Software Configuration Management***
    - *Software Configuration Management Process*
    - *Release Management*

EXERCISES

Multiple Choice Questions

5.1 The unit of effort is

(a) Days (b) Months (c) Hours (d) Person-months

5.2 The metric which considers algorithm complexity while estimating the size is

(a) Feature point (b) Function point (c) KLOC (d) KDSI

5.3 In one of the following COCOMO models, effort is estimated as a function of the number of kilo lines of code

(a) Basic (b) Intermediate (c) Detailed (d) Advanced

5.4 In an activity network representation, the time required to complete the project is given by

(a) Minimum time (MT)
(b) Latest Finish time (LFT)
(c) Early Finish time (EFT)
(d) Latest Start time (LST)

5.5 _______ is the time that delays a task without changing the total time of the project

(a) Actual (b) Slack (c) Surprlus (d) Latest time

5.6 One of the tools that is used for resource planning is

(a) Critical path (b) Gantt chart
(c) Star UML (d) COCOMO

5.7 The activity that is carried out after the delivery of the product to the customer is

(a) Software maintenance (b) Software engineering
(c) Cost estimation (d) Schedule estimation

Answers of Multiple Choice Questions
5.1 (d), 5.2(a), 5.3(a), 5.4(a), 5.5(b), 5.6(b), 5.7(a)

Short and Long Answer Type Questions

5.1 What is Software Project Management? Explain

5.2 What are a project manager's responsibilities in each software development phase? Justify

5.3 What is software planning? Why is it needed

5.4 What are the different ways to estimate the Lines of code of a software system

5.5 What is a function point metric? What are its drawbacks

5.6 What is software maintenance? What are the different types of maintenance

5.7 What is software configuration management? Why is it needed

5.8 Explain how versions are maintained for various software configuration items

5.9 Describe the process of change management

5.10 What is release planning? How it helps the project manager in managing the releases

5.11 A 70,000 LOC system software is to be developed. Assume that the cost of the developer is Rs.32000/= per month and other overhead cost is Rs. 56000/=, estimate the cost of the project. Also, estimate the time for development.

5.12 A 35600 LOC application project is available in the market for Rs. 60,000/=. Is it feasible to develop the project or purchase it assuming that the developer cost is Rs. 28,000/= p.m.

5.13 The given table indicates the task in a project, activities, dependencies, and the time taken for completion of each activity. Draw a activity network and identify the critical path. Generate the Gantt chart.

Task Name	Duration (weeks)	Predecessor
T_1	5	-
T_2	5	-
T_3	3	T_1
T_4	5	T_2
T_5	4	T_3
T_6	3	T_3, T_4
T_7	9	T_2, T_5, T_6
T_8	13	T_7
T_9	18	T_8
T_{10}	11	T_9

PRACTICAL

5.1 Perform W^5HH analysis on the following systems and store the document on any of the project management tools
(a) Banking System (b) Railway reservation System (c) Online Shopping System

5.2 Identify activities for each of the following systems, then suggest a work breakdown structure, draw network activity diagram, Gantt chart and find the critical path. Create these projects on GI or any other project management tool.
(a) Railway reservation System (b) Online Shopping System.

5.3 Consider any mini-project. Maintain the Software Configuration Items on GIT or any other tool. Whenever changes are made to the system, ensure that GIT is updated regularly.

KNOW MORE

Project management is a set of guiding principles and approaches to effectively manage the software project to deliver quality products within the given timelines and estimated budget. A project manager adds value to the organization through effective planning, budgeting, and control of activities. Effective monitoring and control are possible if an accurate software plan is available.

Once the requirements specification is available and the scope of the system is defined correctly, the effort, time for development, cost, and staff required are estimated. Each model or technique is only accurate for estimation as the projects have different levels of complexity, and the resources required may vary from one project to another. The effort estimation can also be done using empirical techniques such as Expert Judgement and Delphi Cost Estimation. Experts estimate the project's cost through experience in the expert judgment technique. Sometimes, they take the estimation of a similar project as a base, and based on the additional validations, if any, the cost is included, and inflation cost is added to get the resultant cost. This technique may suffer from personal bias and erroneous estimates. A Delphi cost estimation technique is used to overcome the expert judgment approach's drawbacks.

In the Delphi technique, the estimation is carried out by a team of experts and a coordinator. In this technique, the coordinator provides all estimators with a copy of the software requirements specification and an estimation form. Each member will make individual estimates and submit them to the coordinator. The coordinator prepares a summary of feedback on the submitted estimate and returns it back to the members to re-estimate. This process is iterated until an acceptable estimate arrives and the coordinator prepares the final estimate.

In release planning, each story is divided into tasks, and the effort required by each task is estimated. The releases are planned based on the priority of the story. Project planning and release planning are essential to manage and control the activities. Each item produced during the development phase is a configuration item. These items may require changes. Hence, each configuration item requires versioning. The reasons for change are also documented and stored in a configuration repository. In order to ensure that the changes are correctly realized, delivered on time, and within budget to the customer's satisfaction, configuration auditing is required regularly.

REFERENCES AND SUGGESTED READINGS

- Sommerville, I. (2016). Software Engineering. 10th Edition, Pearson Education Limited, Boston
- Roger S. Pressman (2010). Software Engineering: A Practitioner's Approach, McGraw-Hill
- Rajib Mall (2018). Fundamentals of Software Engineering, 5th Edition, PHI Learning Private Limited.
- Pankaj Jalote (2010). Software Engineering: A Precise Approach, Wiley-India
- Bob Hughes, Mike Cotterell (2005). Software Project Management, 2nd Edition, The McGraw- Hill Companies.
- IEEE Standard for Software Project Management Plans (1058-1998)

Dynamic QR Code for Further Reading

REFERENCES FOR FURTHER LEARNING

- Sommerville, I. (2016) Software Engineering. 10th Edition, Pearson Education Limited, Boston
- Roger S. Pressman (2010) Software Engineering: A Practitioner's Approach, McGraw-Hill
- Rajib Mall (2018), Fundamentals of Software Engineering, 5th Edition, PHI Learning Private Limited.
- Pankaj Jalote (2010), Software Engineering: A Precise Approach, Wiley-India.
- Grady Booch, James Rumbaugh, Ivar Jacobson (2017), The Unified Modeling Language User Guide, 2nd Edition, Pearson India Education Services Pvt. Ltd.
- IEEE Recommended Practice for Software Requirements Specifications (830-1993/1998.
- IEEE Recommended Practice for Software Design Descriptions (1016-1998).
- Srinivasan Desikan, Gopalaswamy Ramesh(2011). Software Testing Principles and Practices, Pearson-Education
- K.K. Aggarwal, Yogesh Singh(2008). Software Engineering, New Age International Publishers.
- IEEE Recommended Practice for Software Design Descriptions (1016-1998).
- Bob Hughes, Mike Cotterell (2005). Software Project Management, 2nd Edition, The McGraw- Hill Companies.
- IEEE Standard for Software Project Management Plans (1058-1998)
- Richard Fairley(2017). Software Engineering Concepts, McGraw Hill Education.
- James Peters, Witold Pedcryz (2007). Software Engineering : An Engineering Approach, Wiley.
- IEEE Standard for Configuration Management in Systems and Software Engineering (828-2012)

CO AND PO ATTAINMENT TABLE

Course outcomes (COs) for this course can be mapped with the programme outcomes (POs) after the completion of the course and a correlation can be made for the attainment of POs to analyze the gap. After proper analysis of the gap in the attainment of POs necessary measures can be taken to overcome the gaps.

Table for CO and PO attainment

Course Outcomes	Attainment of Programme Outcomes (1- Weak Correlation; 2- Medium correlation; 3- Strong Correlation)						
	PO-1	PO-2	PO-3	PO-4	PO-5	PO-6	PO-7
CO-1							
CO-2							
CO-3							
CO-4							
CO-5							

The data filled in the above table can be used for gap analysis.

INDEX